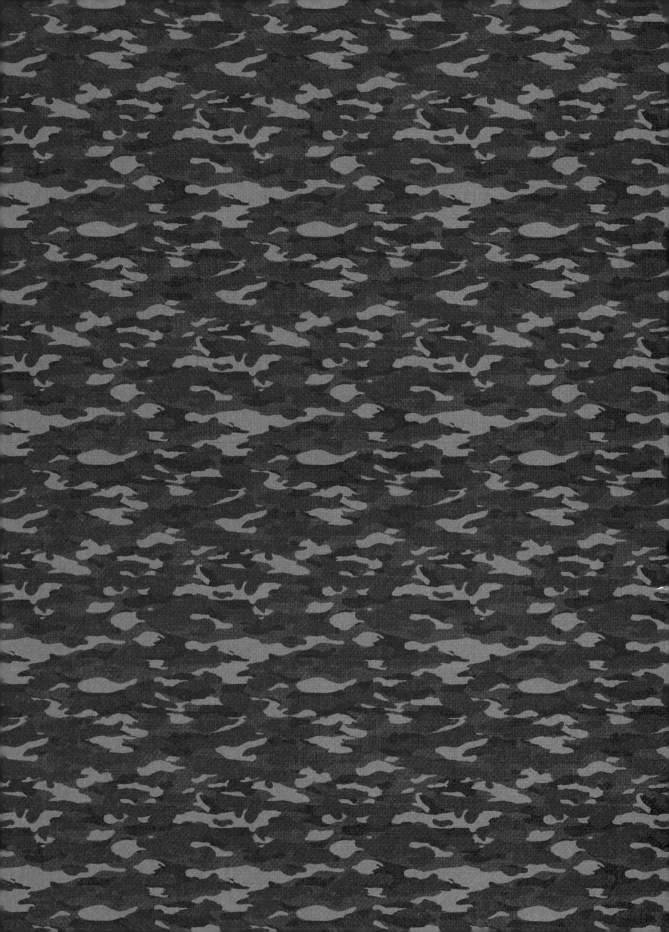

WILD
MEAT

WILD MEAT

The complete guide to cooking game

Ross O'Meara

Hardie Grant

BOOKS

CONTENTS

INTRODUCTION

People have hunted for thousands of years. It's a skill that a few have kept, but most of us have lost due to the way our lives are lived these days. In the past, a hunt, when successful, was a celebration, as it meant survival for another day – or even better, preparation for the winter and lean times ahead.

I wasn't born into a hunting family. Dad is from country Australia and Mum is from the city. I was drawn to hunting over the years, by following my food chain as a chef, in an attempt to get to the roots of where my food came from. My godfather, Lyall Crockford, was the major influence in getting me started with hunting. And good friend Alex Zacharewicz (aka 'The Russian') mentored me into the hunter I am today.

These days, many of us eat meat that we are not connected to. A lot of people won't ever realise where it came from, or how it came onto their plates.

As a chef, I was dealing with produce every day, but then I started to break it down. I wanted to know how everything I was using in the kitchen was produced, from cheese to charcuterie and preserves, and that then led me to protein. I wanted to know why great pork was great, and what made a good chicken good. Why is wild game so much better than farmed game? The main difference is in how you harvest it, and the environment you take it from.

I had a time in my life when I took full responsibility for my family's food production. For 10 years, we had a small-hold farm on Bruny Island, off southern Tasmania, where we raised and harvested all our own protein. And since I am a bad gardener, we swapped vegies for meat. We raised old-breed, free-range pigs, which I processed into old-style charcuterie, and some we sold as fresh pork. We had just enough sheep to keep the paddock under control, and some goats for a while, until they got the better of us. Chickens were great for eggs and the odd dinner, and partridge came and went. Then I would hunt for deer, rabbits, possum, hare and goats.

When I first started hunting, I called myself a game harvester, as I looked at game only as meat that I was accessing for my own consumption, or for commercial sale. These days, I consider myself a hunter, as I am more inclined to manage the areas I hunt. I don't have the need to take just any animal that I see, and I now feed my family and others with the meat that I harvest in the field. As hunters, I feel we have a responsibility to sustain this resource for future generations.

North America has implemented great hunting management with their tag system, which helps with the conservation of species and keeps the wildlife abundant. I haven't made the trip to hunt over there yet, but hope to visit soon. Europe, with its deeply embedded hunting traditions and history, has also managed to keep hunting sustainable as a food source.

Australia has many environmentally damaging introduced species that need to be controlled, as well as a few native species – but we need to start actually using this protein, rather than culling and simply leaving it. Most Australians would hate to admit it, but New Zealand is so far in front of us when it comes to game management, with New Zealanders having embraced the hunting–harvesting lifestyle and utilising its game as a resource.

'I THINK, BACK THEN, IT WOULD'VE BEEN [MORE] ABOUT THE PRODUCT, WHICH IS THE WAY WE'RE TURNING THESE DAYS. PEOPLE ARE RELYING ON BETTER-QUALITY MEAT AND DOING AS LITTLE AS POSSIBLE TO IT.'

As a hunter with a food background, I have compiled this book of wild game recipes with the idea of also giving hunters, from novices to old hands, knowledge about the breakdown of the animals they harvest in the field. Some will have their own methods and may not agree with what I have put down in these pages, but there are so many ways to approach field harvesting to get the same result. I don't declare myself to be an expert, but I have worked with food all my working life, and I take an approach that I hope many will find accessible.

The recipes themselves are very approachable, with a strong theme of making things from scratch. I have also linked the selected animal species covered in this book with similar or comparable species from other parts of the world to substitute in the recipes.

As hunters, we are custodians of the bush. There may be a bit of earnestness in my words, but I do believe that the more we take responsibility for the meat we eat, and for our whole food chain generally, the better off we will all be. And what better than free-range, cruelty-free, organic, hormone-free, grass-fed protein, which helps keep our natural ecosystems in balance and conserve our parks and wild lands around the globe.

Ready for the hunt

Sambar deer grazing

GLOSSARY

1 **Backfat**
The top layer of fat of a pig, starting at the neck and finishing at the shoulders.

2 **Bakers flour**
This type of flour has a higher protein content than regular flour. It is also known as 'strong' flour or 'bread' flour.

3 **Caping**
Refers to the act of skinning an animal for a trophy mount.

4 **Caul fat**
The fat that surrounds the internal organs of animals. It is also called lace fat and crépinette. In Europe, it is used to keep meat moist during cooking and roasting. If you can't get it, you can use streaky bacon or prosciutto.

5 **Cultured butter**
Butter that has had the cream fermented before the churning process, resulting in a richer and more tangy flavour.

6 **Dressing**
The act of removing the pelt or skin from a carcass.

7 **Lard**
Rendered-down animal fat, which is widely available in supermarkets these days.

8 **Pure sea salt**
Less refined than table salt, pure sea salt doesn't contain anti-caking agents.

9 **Salt, for seasoning**
As a golden rule, the perfect amount of salt for burgers, fresh sausages and any farce or meat paste is simply adding 1% salt to the overall weight of the fresh meat mixture.

10 **Setting overnight**
Leaving a carcass to 'set' overnight allows the meat to lose a little moisture and the proteins in the meat to firm up.

11 **The pluck**
The heart, liver and lungs of a carcass.

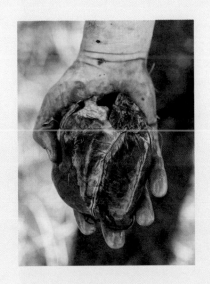

Preparing quail

COOKING & PRESERVATION TIPS

Here's a quick round-up of most of the items you'll need to tackle the wonders of fire cooking, hot and cold smoking, vacuum sealing and meat packing – with a few general tips and terms thrown in for good measure. Once you start with these basics, you will see what you will need for your own individual set-up, and what works best for you.

Handy kitchen items

Basting brush
Any catering brush that is suitable for brushing a marinade or sauce over food during cooking.

Cartouche
A simple, temporary 'lid' made from a sheet of baking paper, used to cover a pot or frying pan during simmering.

Digital scales
A set of electronic scales is useful for weighing out precise quantities, especially when making charcuterie and the like. They are very inexpensive and widely available these days.

Meat thermometer
A small thermometer used for checking the internal temperature of meat during or after cooking, to check for doneness.

Pastry brush
Any catering brush that is used to brush baked goods with an egg wash or other glaze.

Fire cooking is a fantastic way to prepare game meat

The smoker ready for cooking

Fire cooking

Solid cast-iron pans and pots
When you cook directly on a fire, you need solid cast-iron cookware, as the fierce heat will warp or even burn the lightest steel.

Tripod or grill stand
This lets you position your cookware a good distance from the fire, so you can control the heat that you are cooking on.

Long tongs
Having a set of long, good-quality tongs to turn or handle the meat will ensure you don't burn your fingers or hands when you're close to the fire.

Dry thick cloths or leather gloves
Always use these to protect and insulate your hands when cooking over hot coals or flames. Avoid wet or thin cloths, as these conduct heat and will easily burn you.

Hot & cold smoking

Hot and cold smoking have been used to preserve meat since the dawn of time.

There are so many different brands and types of smokers on the market, and they all will do one or both types of smoking. I prefer to use wood-fuel smokers and not the pellet variety. I am not fussed about the size or shape of the smoker, as I have worked a large off-set smoker that was from an old railway boiler that weighed just less than 5 tonnes (5½ tons), down to the stand-up small home models that will take only a few kilograms of meat. I love the way that once it is lit, you are at the mercy of the fire – and you spend the next 12 hours or so trying to control it.

The main difference between hot and cold smoking is the temperature. Cold smoking temperatures range from 30–70°C (86–158°F), with hot smoking ranging from 70–110°C (158–230°F). If you start going over the 110°C (230°F) mark, then you are pit roasting!

The type of wood you use is another factor when smoking – in terms of the particular variety, and its size (whether large, or shavings). I tend to use Australian hardwood, and sometimes fruit trees, but I have also used wine barrels. The base cure and/or rub you use on the meat before you smoke it will also guide the outcome. With smoking, I have always let the meat talk and kept the rubs and cures quite basic.

Smoking is an endlessly variable way of preserving meat, and you might not get the result you want straight away – but when you do, it's bliss.

Vacuum sealing & packing

This is another way to extend the shelf life of meat. You will need:

- a chambered food vacuum-packing machine or vacuum sealer (see below)
- good-quality vacuum packing/sealing bags
- a marker pen for labelling the sealed packets.

Food vacuum-packing and sealing machines are very helpful when storing and freezing meat, especially if you don't have a cool room set-up, or access to a fridge large enough to hang a whole animal in.

For instance, I break down an animal in the field, transport it home and let the meat's core temperature cool down and the protein 'set' overnight. The next day I will trim all the meat into cuts and package it using my vacuum-packing machine. I'll then place it in the fridge and let it rest for 2 weeks. After that I repack the meat if there is a bag full of blood around the cuts, and then either freeze the meat for longer storage, or leave it in the fridge if I'm going to use it within the next couple of weeks.

I am lucky enough to still have my vacuum-packing machine from my farm processing days. The main difference between home vacuum sealers and a vacuum-packing machine is that home vacuum sealers suck air out of the packet, whereas a vacuum-packing machine pumps in carbon dioxide, which expels oxygen – and less oxygen trapped in the packet means a better shelf life.

For this reason, vacuum-packing machines will give you a longer shelf life than a home vacuum sealer. With a vacuum-packing machine, I find frozen cuts will easily last 6–12 months if the seal of the bag hasn't broken. (I have even had frozen cuts dating over 2 years, and they were still fine – though I would not recommend freezing them this long.) In the fridge, the cuts should last up to 6–8 weeks without spoiling.

With a home vacuum sealer, I have found the cuts will last just as well in the freezer, but only up to 4 weeks in the fridge.

The really fancy vacuum-packing machines can be hooked up to nitrogen, giving an even longer shelf life. This can add months to the use-by date. With some models, the sealed goods can even be classified as shelf stable – meaning no refrigeration is needed.

A good-quality vacuum sealer will stop freezer burn, which is your main concern when you are freezing meat. This is when your seal breaks and the cold air in the freezer comes in direct contact with the meat, drying up the outside of the meat and making it inedible.

Some people try to age meat in a vacuum sealer, but this is against its intended purpose, which is to slow the ageing process right down. If you have the meat too long in the bag – let's say 12 weeks – gases can build up from the meat breaking down and not being able to be released. This will taint the meat, giving off a bad smell when opening the bag.

A rabbit ready for skinning and butchering

‡ **NOTE**
One of the main things you must remember when packing and storing meat is to label and date each package clearly, so you can keep track of the shelf life and check it hasn't been stored for too long. That way, if you are pulling meat out of the freezer or fridge for a barbecue or meal, you will be rewarded with quality meat, and won't be disappointed to find that it has spoiled.

RECIPES

N.01

GAME BIRDS

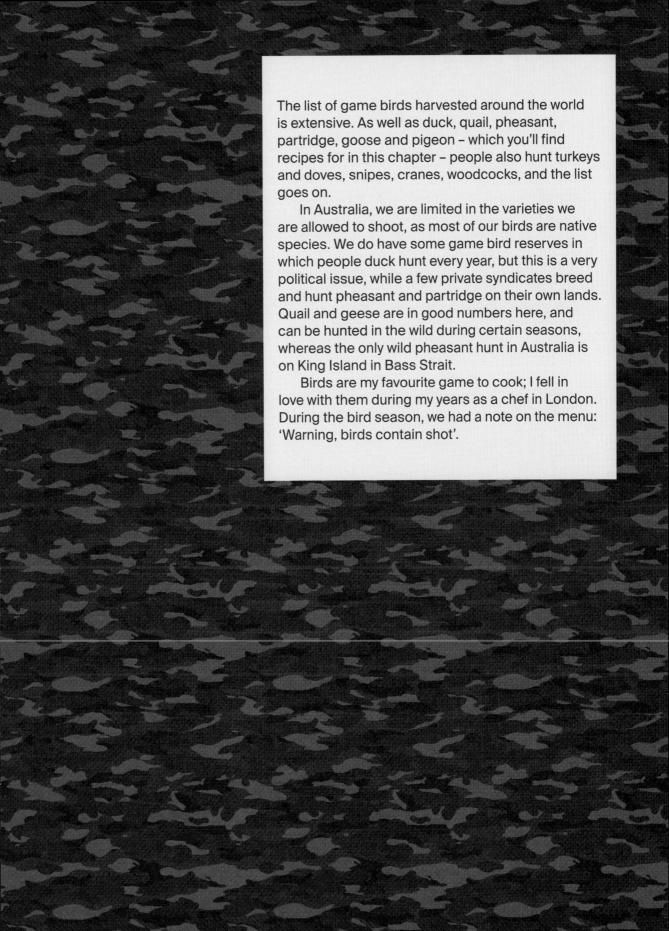

The list of game birds harvested around the world is extensive. As well as duck, quail, pheasant, partridge, goose and pigeon – which you'll find recipes for in this chapter – people also hunt turkeys and doves, snipes, cranes, woodcocks, and the list goes on.

In Australia, we are limited in the varieties we are allowed to shoot, as most of our birds are native species. We do have some game bird reserves in which people duck hunt every year, but this is a very political issue, while a few private syndicates breed and hunt pheasant and partridge on their own lands. Quail and geese are in good numbers here, and can be hunted in the wild during certain seasons, whereas the only wild pheasant hunt in Australia is on King Island in Bass Strait.

Birds are my favourite game to cook; I fell in love with them during my years as a chef in London. During the bird season, we had a note on the menu: 'Warning, birds contain shot'.

GAME BIRDS

LIST OF CUTS

1 Breasts, crown rack
roasting

2 Legs
confit
roasting
braising

3 Boned breast
grilling
roasting

4 Spatchcocked
barbecuing
roasting
grilling
smoking low and slow

5 Whole boned
galantine
roulade

GRILLED DUCK LIVERS WITH SPELT & NETTLES

I was lucky enough to celebrate my 40th birthday at a friend's restaurant, where chef David Moyle made a vego dish for my wife Emma. He prepared a nettle and spelt risotto, and I have never had a dish stick in my mind for as long as that one has. Luckily enough, he was happy to share his recipe – and I've found the only way to make it better is to add duck livers!

You can find stinging nettles growing wild in most fields that have had cattle grazing in them. When you pick them, just remember to wear gloves. They are known as stinging nettles for a reason: the little fur prickles on them will get into your skin and itch like crazy. The flavour of stinging nettles is unique. They taste like they look – 'green', with a slight peppery after-flavour that is a bit like rocket (arugula).

SERVES 4

1 French shallot

1 garlic clove, sliced

200 ml (7 fl oz) grapeseed oil

500 g (1 lb 2 oz) stinging nettles, picked

1.25 litres (42 fl oz/5 cups) chicken stock

400 g (14 oz/2 cups) spelt grains, parboiled for 10 minutes

50 g (1¾ oz) cultured butter

20 ml (¾ fl oz) lemon juice

8 duck livers, trimmed

20 nettle leaves, toasted (see note)

In a heavy-based pot, sweat the shallot and garlic in the oil over a low heat for about 5 minutes until transparent.

Crank the heat up to high and add the nettles. The nettles need to fry quite heavily, so resist the urge to add any liquid too early. Frying the leaves extracts the chlorophyll into the oil, keeping the sauce vibrant; if the nettles are just boiled in the liquid, the sauce will be brown and listless.

Once the nettle leaves begin to disintegrate, add 250 ml (8½ fl oz/1 cup) of the stock and boil aggressively for about 1 minute. Transfer to a strong upright blender and purée. Season with salt and pepper and set aside.

Rinse the spelt grains once in a colander, then add to a heavy-based pot with a snug-fitting lid. Add 1 litre (34 fl oz/4 cups) water. Leaving the lid off, bring to the boil for 10 minutes, then turn the heat down to a rolling simmer for a further 10 minutes.

Remove from the heat and set aside to rest for 10 minutes with the lid on. Spoon the spelt onto a tray and fluff the grains up with a wooden spoon to cool down.

Bring the remaining 1 litre (34 fl oz/4 cups) stock to the boil, then add the spelt. Simmer gently for about 4 minutes, before adding about 250 ml (8½ fl oz/1 cup) of the nettle sauce, or as much as you like, really. (Any remaining nettle sauce can be used in a pasta sauce or soup, or even spiced up for a dressing.)

Stir in the butter and lemon juice, and season with more salt and more pepper than you think it needs.

To finish, season the duck livers, then sauté in a frying pan for 2 minutes on each side and leave to rest for 2 minutes.

Serve the duck livers on top of the spelt, topped with the toasted nettle leaves.

‡ **NOTE**
To toast the nettle leaves, spray them with rice bran oil, spread them out on a heavy baking tray and toast in a preheated 120°C (250°F) oven for 14 minutes.

PIGEON HEARTS ON A STICK

Heart is such tasty meat, once you get over the fact that it is heart – and this is one of those dishes that can convert those who are hesitant or squeamish. Grilling them on skewers makes hearts look like any other meat, making them more familiar and less confronting. Pigeon hearts are very small, which also helps dial down the intimidation factor. You could use any bird hearts here, or even slice bigger ones into bite-sized pieces.

This is another dish I like to cook over coals; a little Japanese hibachi grill works great for this.

SERVES 4 AS TAPAS

4 bamboo skewers or rosemary sprigs
20 pigeon hearts
2 teaspoons rice bran oil
100 g (3½ oz) Chimichurri (page 207)

Soak the bamboo skewers in water for about 15 minutes, so they don't burn on the grill.

Meanwhile, get your hibachi grill coals nice and hot, which will usually take about 30 minutes. If you don't have a coal barbecue, a grill pan or flat barbecue plate will do fine.

Slide five pigeon hearts onto each bamboo stick (or use rosemary sprigs instead), making sure you keep the hearts facing the same way so they will cook evenly. Brush the hearts with the rice bran oil and season generously with salt and pepper.

Place the skewers on the hot hibachi and grill for 5–7 minutes, turning constantly to even out the colour.

Once cooked, remove the skewers and leave to rest for 3 minutes.

Dress with the chimichurri dressing, serving some extra dressing on the side for those who want more.

PIGEON BISTEEYA

A bisteeya is a North African sweet and savoury filo pie with almonds and spices. I make a vegetarian version of this dish most of the time, but traditionally it is made with pigeon or poultry. It's a very special dish to present at the table, when you would create the final scoring with a hot barbecue skewer. The smell of the caramelising cinnamon and sugar is a real showstopper. You will need a round pie dish, about 5 cm (2 in) deep, with a 25 cm (10 in) diameter, that you can heat from underneath and also put in the oven.

SERVES 12

150 g (5½ oz) cultured butter

1 brown onion, thinly sliced

3 garlic cloves, crushed

4 pigeons, cut into sauté pieces

1 litre (34 fl oz/4 cups) Game stock (page 210) or chicken stock

1 tablespoon ground cumin

1 tablespoon ground coriander

5 saffron threads, activated (see note on page 49)

1½ teaspoons ground cinnamon

150 g (5½ oz) fresh filo pastry sheets

5 free-range eggs

100 g (3½ oz) flaked almonds, toasted

1 tablespoon icing (confectioners') sugar

Preheat the oven to 160°C (320°F).

Heat half the butter in a large flameproof casserole dish over a medium heat. Add the onion and garlic and cook slowly for 3 minutes.

Turn up the heat and add the pigeon pieces, making sure you give them a good seasoning with salt and pepper. Brown the pieces on both sides.

Add the stock, followed by the cumin, coriander, saffron and 1 teaspoon of the cinnamon. Bring to the boil, then cover with a cartouche (see page 14) and place in the oven for 45 minutes, or until the pigeon is cooked; the meat should come away from the bone easily.

Pull the dish out of the oven and leave to cool down. Remove all the pigeon pieces and strip the meat away from the bones; place the meat in a bowl and set aside. Strain the stock remaining in the dish and reserve for the custard.

Melt the remaining butter to use for the filo pastry. You must work quickly with the filo so it doesn't dry out, keeping any sheets you are not using under a damp tea towel. Brush some butter in the base of a 25 cm (10 in) round pie dish, about 5 cm (2 in) deep. Layer the filo in the base of the dish, brushing a little melted butter between each sheet and using about seven sheets. When placing the pastry sheets, make sure there is enough pastry to come back over the top to cover the pie. Cover the whole pie dish with a damp tea towel and set aside.

Heat the reserved stock so it is hot, but not boiling. In a large bowl, beat the eggs to combine, then slowly add the hot stock, stirring constantly. Once combined, stir the pigeon meat through.

Scatter a layer of almonds into the pie dish, over the pastry base. Spoon the filling mixture over the almonds. Fold the overhanging pastry over the top, to fully enclose the pie.

Slowly heat the base of the pie dish over a low heat, to colour the base of the filo pastry; this will become the presentation side. This should take about 3–5 minutes. Be very careful, as the filo can burn very quickly – use a spatula to gently lift up one side to have a look and check.

Transfer the pie dish to the oven and bake for 25–30 minutes, until the pastry is golden and stiff to touch. Remove the pie from the oven and let it rest for 3 minutes.

Place a heatproof serving plate over the top and carefully invert the pie dish, so that the pastry base is facing upright.

Combine the icing sugar and remaining ½ teaspoon cinnamon and, using a sieve, dust it over the top of pie.

Heat up a metal barbecue skewer over a gas flame and burn a criss-cross or lattice pattern into the top. Serve straight away, with a carrot salad.

31

POT-ROASTED PARTRIDGE WITH BEANS & BACON

Partridge was one of the first game birds I had the pleasure of cooking in a restaurant. I didn't realise then how lucky I was using field-shot partridge, pheasant, woodcock and snipe. The best way to cook any of these birds is whole and on the bone, to be carved at the table. When you cook a bird on the bone, you get a sweeter meat, and it also helps to keep the bird moist.

For this dish, you'll need to soak the beans the night before.

SERVES 4

butter and oil, for cooking

4 dressed partridges (see note)

8 French shallots, peeled but kept whole

3 garlic cloves, crushed

1 carrot, diced

1 leek, white part only, diced

1 celery stalk, diced

200 g (7 oz) belly bacon (page 176), diced

100 g (3½ oz/½ cup) dried haricot beans, soaked overnight

1 litre (34 fl oz/4 cups) Game stock (page 210)

Preheat the oven to 180°C (350°F).

Heat some butter and oil in a large flameproof casserole dish over a high heat. Season the partridges generously with salt and pepper, then sear them on both breasts for about 3 minutes. Once seared, remove the birds and set aside.

Add the shallots, garlic, carrot, leek, celery and bacon to the dish and sauté for 3 minutes. Add the beans and stock and bring to the boil, then reduce the heat to a slow simmer and place the lid on.

Place the dish in the oven and cook for 15–20 minutes, or until the beans are al dente.

Remove from the oven and add the partridges. Put the lid back on and bake for 20–30 minutes (depending on their size). To check the birds are done, give them a slight squeeze where the thigh meets the leg. If the meat gives way and breaks off the bone, the birds are ready.

Once done, remove the dish from the oven. Leave the birds to rest for 15 minutes with the lid off before serving. A fresh green salad would go well with this dish.

‡ NOTE
A 'dressed' bird is one that has been plucked, drawn (innards removed) and trussed (tied into shape), ready for roasting.

32

GOOSE BAKED IN SALT CRUST

Salt-crust baking is a great way of cooking as it gently steams and bakes at the same time. It works well with game birds, adding a unique flavour as they steam in their own juices. You can also use this technique with a venison haunch for a spectacular table centrepiece.

SERVES 6

oil, for cooking

1 goose, dressed for the oven (see note, opposite)

flour, for dusting

3 garlic cloves, crushed

50 g (1¾ oz) cultured butter

2 rosemary sprigs

2 thyme sprigs

SALT-CRUST DOUGH

600 g (1 lb 5 oz/4 cups) plain (all-purpose) flour

400 g (14 oz) salt

4 egg whites

250 ml (8½ fl oz/1 cup) water

To make the dough, combine the flour and salt in a bowl, stir in the egg whites and add the water until it forms a stiff dough. Cover with a damp tea towel and set aside to rest for 30 minutes.

Meanwhile, oil the goose, then sear it on all sides in a large hot frying pan over a medium–high heat. Make sure you only oil the goose, not the pan, and don't be shy with the seasoning. Place the goose in a roasting tin and leave to rest for 15 minutes.

Once rested, truss the bird naturally, by cutting a 3 cm (1¼ in) hole in the skin of the shin of the back leg, and tucking the other leg through that hole. Then fold each wing under the bird, to keep the sides tucked in.

Preheat the oven to 200°C (400°F).

Roll the pastry out on a floured bench, into an oval that is 38 cm (15 in) wide, 50 cm (19½ in) long and 1 cm (½ in) thick. Place the goose in the centre, breast side up, and tuck the garlic and butter under the skin. Place the herbs on top and fold up the dough to encase the goose. Seal the edges by pressing together well.

Carefully lift the goose and place in a sturdy roasting tin. Bake in the oven for 1½ hours.

Remove from the oven and leave to rest for 20 minutes, before breaking the crust and serving. I like to serve this dish with a good selection of old-school roast vegies, such as potato, celeriac, turnip, swede (rutabaga) and carrot.

‡ NOTE

This dish can be cooked in a camp oven, if you feel the need to eat outdoors around a fire. Just place the goose, in its salt-crust dough, into your camp oven, put the lid on, and make sure you cover the top with coals. It should take 3–4 hours to cook, and I'd let it sit for 30 minutes before tapping into the crust.

CRISPY FIVE-SPICE GOOSE

This dish makes a great little share plate to hand around. The flavour is sharp and intense, and keeps you coming back for more. In this recipe I have used the breast off the bone, but you can use any part of the bird with the bone in, if that's the way you want to roll.

SERVES 6 AS A SHARED PLATE

2 free-range eggs
1 garlic clove, crushed
2 magpie goose breasts, skin off
1 tablespoon five-spice
175 g (6 oz) plain (all-purpose) flour
1 tablespoon baking powder
1 teaspoon sea salt flakes
1–2 teaspoons white pepper
rice bran oil, for shallow-frying

Crack the eggs into a bowl and beat them. Add the garlic and a tablespoon of water to help break up the egg.

Slice the goose breasts as thinly as you can. Place in the egg mixture and stir around until the meat strips are well coated. Set aside.

In another bowl, mix together the five-spice, flour, baking powder, salt and white pepper.

Heat a heavy-based frying pan filled with 1 cm (½ in) of oil to 175°C (345°F). Take the goose out of the egg, strip by strip, dust in the flour mixture and place on a plate, ready for frying.

You can check the oil is hot enough by placing the end of one of the goose strips in the oil – if it starts sizzling, it's ready to go.

Add only enough goose strips as will fit into the pan without overcrowding, and fry for 2 minutes each side. It might take two or three batches before they are all done, so you can leave the fried ones in a very low oven to keep them warm.

Rest the strips on paper towel for 2 minutes before serving.

‡ NOTE
If you'd like to make a main dish out of this, it pairs well with a cucumber and dill salad.

PHEASANT CABBAGE ROLL

Again I am stealing a dish, this time one I used to serve in a restaurant when I worked in London – but I don't know if the head chef, Konrad Melling, stole it from someone else. I love how this dish is self-complete, and looks like you have some serious cooking skills, but is actually really simple to make. And you use the whole bird, bones and all.

SERVES 4

1 savoy cabbage

4 pheasants, boned, separated into legs and breasts

butter and oil, for cooking

1 carrot, finely diced

1 leek, white part only, finely diced

1 celery stalk, finely diced

2 garlic cloves, crushed

2 thyme sprigs

1 rosemary sprig

1 litre (34 fl oz/4 cups) Game stock (page 210)

Put a stockpot or large saucepan filled with water on to boil.

Meanwhile, pull off and reserve the leaves from the cabbage, picking the leaves down to the heart or core, which should be about the size of your fist. Dice the cabbage heart as finely as possible and set aside.

Once the water is boiling, add a good handful of salt, then the outside separated cabbage leaves. Once the water has come back to the boil, strain the leaves off, then cool them down in iced water. Once cooled, shake the water off the leaves and place them in between several tea towels to soak up the extra moisture.

Place the boned pheasant legs in a food processor and blend until they form a paste; this should take about 1–2 minutes. Set aside.

Place a frying pan over a high heat and add some butter and oil. Add the diced cabbage and other vegetables, along with the garlic and herbs. Sauté for 3–4 minutes, then set aside to cool. Once cooled, add to the processed leg meat. Season with salt and pepper and place in the fridge until ready to use.

‡ CONTINUED →

Grab a stainless steel bowl with a diameter of 24–28 cm (9½–11 in) and line it with a tea towel big enough to fit the bowl and hang over the side. Don't use your best linen, as it will be cooking in stock for a few hours – or you can use muslin (cheesecloth).

Layer the bowl with some cabbage leaves, making sure they are spread out and not overlapping much. Now season the layer with salt and pepper, then spread on some of the sautéed pheasant leg mixture, to a thickness of 1 cm (½ in). Continue this process until the mixture and the cabbage leaves are used up.

Grab the sides of the tea towel and bring them into the middle, then start to twist the top, so it brings up the sides of the cabbage to form a ball. Once you have your ball shape, tie the top with kitchen string.

Place the ball in a pot deep enough to cover the ball with stock. Pour in the stock and bring it to the boil, then turn the heat down to a slow simmer and cook for 1–1½ hours. Check to see if it is cooked by pressing on the cabbage ball; it should be solid, with no give in it at all.

Once cooked, remove the cabbage ball, place it on a tray and refrigerate overnight. Strain the stock, then reduce it down to a sauce consistency over a medium heat for about 20–30 minutes, to use on the finished dish.

When ready to serve, take the cold cabbage ball out of the fridge and remove it from the tea towel. Slice it into eight wedges. Place four of the wedges on a flat baking tray. (You will have four pieces left over, for another day.)

Meanwhile, preheat the oven to 200°C (400°F).

Place an ovenproof frying pan over a high heat and add some butter and oil to cook the pheasant breasts. Season both sides of the breasts with salt and pepper, then place them in the pan, skin side down. Cook for 3 minutes on the skin side, then turn the breasts over.

Place the pan in the oven with the tray of cabbage wedges. Bake for 3 minutes, then turn the oven down to 130°C (265°F).

Leave the wedges in the oven, but remove the pheasant breasts and leave to rest for 10 minutes.

Meanwhile, reheat the sauce on the stovetop so it's nice and hot.

Place the warm cabbage wedges on your serving plates. Slice the breasts as thinly as you can, then arrange them down each cabbage wedge. Drizzle the sauce over and serve straight away.

‡ **NOTE**
You'll need to start this dish the day before.

GRILLED QUAIL, FIG & DANDELION GLAZE

Friends that you make from hunting are friends for life. I met Steve through a mutual friend for a red deer hunt. We had a storm the last three days and all the deer were bedded and nothing was around. Since then, we have hunted with success in all species of deer and birds. I'm sure our kids will hunt together with us for years to come.

SERVES 4

QUAIL AND GRILLED FIGS

4 medium quail, plucked, cleaned and butterflied

thyme sprig, chopped

1 garlic clove, crushed

olive oil, to marinate and for brushing

salt, to taste

1 head radicchio, sliced into 8 wedges

6 figs, cut in half

1 bunch flat-leaf (Italian) parsley, chopped

100 g (3½ oz) toasted almonds, chopped

DANDELION REDUCTION

50 g (1¾ oz) dandelion root

50 g (1¾ oz) honey

GLAZE FOR QUAIL

30 g (1 oz) honey

Marinate the quail in thyme, garlic, olive oil and salt for 1½–2 hours.

To make the dandelion reduction, bring 300 ml (10 fl oz) water and the dandelion root to the boil, then turn off the heat and allow to steep for 10 minutes.

Strain the dandelion, discard the root, return the dandelion water to the saucepan, add the honey and bring to a simmer. Reduce the liquid by three-quarters, then allow to cool and set aside.

To make the glaze for the quail, mix the honey with 40 ml (1¼ fl oz) warm water. Set aside for basting the quail.

Get your coal barbecue nice and hot.

Brush the radicchio and figs with olive oil, then grill the radicchio until slightly wilted and the figs until just warmed through.

On a plate, mix the radicchio, figs, chopped parsley and chopped toasted almonds, then dress lightly with the dandelion reduction and season to taste.

Brush the quail with the honey glaze on both sides and grill for 1–2 minutes each side, or until just cooked through. Remove from the heat, allow to rest for 3 minutes, then serve.

OFFAL

Offal (also known as variety meats) has been eaten for centuries all around the world. In Great Britain, Europe, Asia, the Middle East, Africa and South America, offal is still a strong part of the diet because it is so rich in protein, vitamins and minerals, but it has been lost somewhat in other countries.

I feel this has come about from the abundance of prime cuts due to industrial-scale animal farming making meat so cheap. In recent years, there has been a push back towards 'nose to tail' eating, respecting the life of the animal by eating as many parts as possible from the one kill.

When harvesting offal from game animals, you have to be very careful, as the internal organs are the pathway for parasites and disease. In Australia, hydatids, liver fluke, toxoplasmosis and 1080 poison are the most common contaminants you will find in offal.

Some of these diseases are noticeable by eye when looking at the pluck, but some are not. You have to be very knowledgeable about the local environment that you are hunting in. I will only eat offal from select animals that I harvest, as I know the areas that I hunt, and the species I will eat offal from aren't susceptible to disease.

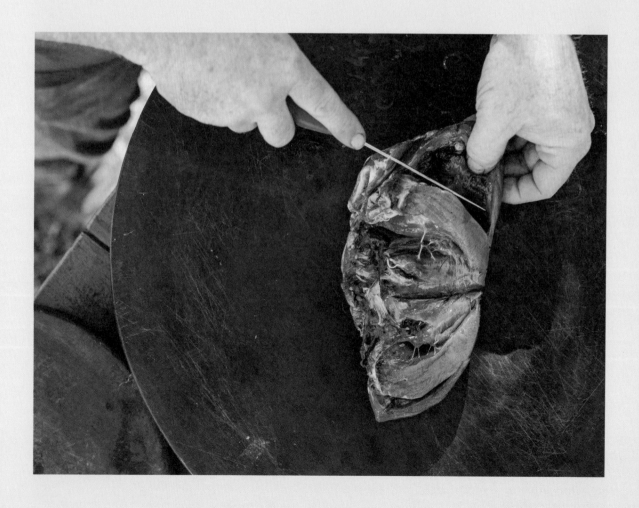

Here is a list of offal I will eat, from species that I harvest.

1 **Birds**
Heart, liver, gizzards

2 **Rabbit & hare**
Heart, liver, kidneys

3 **Possum & squirrel**
I don't eat the offal

4 **Wallaby & kangaroo**
I don't eat the offal

5 **Pig**
Heart, liver, tongue, kidneys – depending on the environment

6 **Goat & sheep**
Heart, liver, tongue, kidneys – depending on the environment

7 **Buffalo, bulls & banteng**
Heart, liver, tongue, kidneys

8 **Deer**
Heart, liver, tongue, kidneys

Venison tongue

‡ **NOTE**
In Australia, 1080 poison is still in use. If you ever come across the pluck of an animal that has a blue colour, do not eat this animal, as it has traces of 1080. Make sure you clean everything that has come in contact with this animal, to avoid accidental cross-contamination or poisoning.

41

Out bush

Wintertime

RABBIT HARE POSSUM & SQUIRREL

Hares and rabbits are plentiful in many areas, adapt to a wide variety of conditions, and reproduce quickly, so hunting is often less regulated than for other varieties of game. In rural areas of North America and particularly in pioneer times, they were a common source of meat. Because of their extremely low fat content, they are a poor choice as a survival food.

RABBIT / HARE

LIST OF CUTS

1 **Backstraps/loin**
   grilling

2 **Back legs**
   slow roasting, braising

3 **Forequarters**
   braising

4 **Sauté cut**
   braising

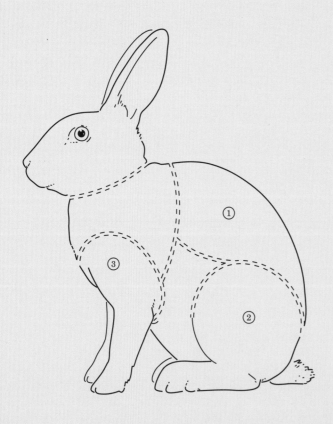

SQUIRREL

LIST OF CUTS

1 Backstraps
grilling

2 Topside
grilling

3 Legs
braising

4 Forequarters
braising

BUSHMAN'S RABBIT RAVIOLI WITH A WARM TOMATO, SAFFRON & CAPER SAUCE

This dish is light, delicate and sublime, with a touch of finesse ... not your average hunter's fare. The 'bushman's' part of this dish is using wonton wrappers as the ravioli sheets, which takes away the effort of rolling fresh pasta and filling the ravioli, with much less mess. Prepare the filling in advance to make the construction of the dish much quicker.

SERVES 4

RABBIT RAVIOLI

butter and oil, for cooking

1 rabbit, about 700 g (1 lb 9 oz), cut into sauté pieces

1–2 brown onions, diced

1 garlic clove, crushed

5 thyme sprigs

100 ml (3½ fl oz) white wine

600 ml (20½ fl oz) Game stock (page 210) or chicken stock

20 square wonton wrappers

pecorino, to serve (optional)

TOMATO, SAFFRON & CAPER SAUCE

1–2 red onions, thinly sliced

2 medium-sized ripe tomatoes

2 tablespoons finely chopped chives

1 tablespoon whole baby capers

a pinch of ground coriander

1 teaspoon saffron threads, activated (see note opposite)

100 ml (3½ fl oz) extra virgin olive oil

juice of 1 lemon

Preheat the oven to 160°C (320°F).

To make the ravioli filling, heat a tablespoon of butter and oil in a flameproof casserole dish over a medium heat. Place the rabbit pieces in a bowl and season generously with salt and pepper. Start cooking the rabbit in the dish. Once both sides are golden, remove the rabbit to a plate to rest.

Add the onion, garlic and thyme to the dish and cook over a low heat for about 10 minutes, until the onion is translucent. Turn the heat up to high, add the wine and stock and bring to the boil.

Add the rabbit pieces, then place the lid on. Transfer to the oven and cook for 2 hours, or until the rabbit meat is coming away from the bone. Set aside to cool.

Once the rabbit has cooled, pick the meat from the bones and lightly shred using your fingers. Strain and save the braising liquid; you can add a bit of the liquid to the shredded rabbit if the meat is a bit dry. Check the seasoning, then place in the fridge.

For the sauce, place the onion in a ceramic or steel bowl, lightly sprinkle with salt and leave for at least 15 minutes. This will add flavour and texture to the onion and remove the bitterness. Quarter the tomatoes and remove the seeds, then dice the flesh and place in a separate bowl to the onion. Add the chives, capers, coriander and saffron to the tomato. Rinse the onion with cold water and squeeze dry by hand, then add to the tomato mixture. Mix in the olive oil and lemon juice, season to taste, then leave to steep at room temperature while cooking the ravioli.

To assemble the ravioli, which is best done near serving time, have a pastry brush and bowl of water handy. Place a row of 10 wonton wrappers on a clean bench. Put a tablespoon of rabbit mixture in the middle of each wrapper, leaving a clear border all around the edge for sealing. Using the brush, wipe the pastry edges with water. Place another wrapper on top of each, sealing around the edges with your fingers.

Find yourself a saucepan large enough to fit all the ravioli. Generously fill the pan with water, add a tablespoon of salt and bring to the boil. Add the ravioli and let the water come back to the boil, then cook for 2–3 minutes, or until they float on top of the water. Remember, you only need to cook the pasta, not the filling.

While the ravioli are cooking, gently heat the sauce in a saucepan, being careful not to boil or overheat the sauce so it doesn't lose its flavour; it only needs to be about 60°C (140°F).

Once the pasta is cooked, drain the ravioli, place on serving plates and top with the sauce. You can add a sprinkling of cheese to this pasta if you wish – I would recommend a pecorino.

‡ NOTE

To 'activate' the saffron and release its aromatic oils, steep it in a splash of hot water for about 15 minutes, or lightly toast it in a dry frying pan.

SEARED HARE LOINS WITH ROSEMARY, BUTTER & VINEGAR SAUCE

This is a field dish, meaning it's a 'one pan over the fire' affair using the spoils of your hunt. The hare loins can be substituted with any game loins or backstraps from your harvest.

SERVES 2

2 hare loins, trimmed
oil, for cooking
1 rosemary sprig
1 garlic clove, crushed
50 g (1¾ oz) butter
50 ml (1¾ fl oz) red wine vinegar

Place a cast-iron skillet over some coals from a fire to heat up. Season the hare loins with salt and black pepper. Once the pan is hot, add the oil and quickly follow with the hare loins. Cook for 2 minutes on one side, then turn and cook on the other side for 1½ minutes.

Add the rosemary and garlic, swirling them in the pan with the loins, then add the butter and vinegar, still swirling the pan so the butter melts and binds to the vinegar.

Remove from the heat and keep moving the pan until you see the sauce start to reduce a bit and thicken. Let it sit for a few minutes to rest before serving. This is campfire cooking at its best, with crusty bread – a hunter's delight.

DEVILLED RABBIT KIDNEYS ON TOAST

Devilled kidneys are a Victorian-era breakfast dish. With my British heritage, I remember eating this dish for breakfast as a kid, but with lamb kidneys. Rabbit kidneys are a bit sweeter in flavour, and small in size, so you need a few rabbits to get a good serving – but you can also add hare or deer kidneys to fill them out.

SERVES 1

10 rabbit kidneys (5 rabbits' worth)

flour, for coating

1 slice sourdough bread

20 g (¾ oz) butter

1 teaspoon Mustard (page 200)

a few shakes of Worcestershire sauce (page 206)

a few shakes of Fermented chilli sauce (page 204)

1 tablespoon chopped flat-leaf (Italian) parsley

To prepare the kidneys, split them lengthways and remove the core on the inside. Then dust the kidneys in flour.

Toast or grill your slice of sourdough and place on your serving plate.

Warm a frying pan over a high heat. Add the butter, then the kidneys. Turn the kidneys after 1 minute, then add the mustard, Worcestershire sauce and chilli sauce and cook for 30 seconds, swirling the pan to mix the sauces.

Once the sauce has combined, add the parsley and season to taste. Serve hot, on your toast.

HARE PITHIVIERS

A pithivier is a traditional French dish hailing from the town of Pithivier – but to the rest of us, it's a puff pastry pie. These are great to eat cold as a snack on your hunt, and this dish can also impress the best at your next dinner party. You can use bought pastry, but the pastry recipe here is for a quick puff that will take the dish to the next level, and can be made the day before. Again, the filling must be made in advance and cooled before use, so the pastry doesn't go soggy.

SERVES 4

QUICK PUFF PASTRY

250 g (9 oz/1⅔ cups) bakers flour

a good pinch of salt

250 g (9 oz) unsalted butter

100 ml (3½ fl oz) cold water

1 egg, whisked, for glazing

FILLING

butter and oil, for cooking

1 hare (1.5–2 kg/3 lb 5 oz–4 lb 6 oz), cut into sauté cuts

flour, for coating

1 French shallot, chopped

3 garlic cloves, crushed

1 carrot, roughly chopped

1 leek, roughly chopped

1 celery stalk, roughly chopped

1 tablespoon tomato purée

50 ml (1¾ fl oz) red wine

475 ml (16 fl oz) Game stock (page 210) or chicken stock

1 thyme and 1 rosemary sprig

To make the pastry, sift the flour and salt into a large bowl. Add the butter and rub it into the flour using your fingers. Don't overdo it; you still want to see chunks of butter. Make a well in the centre, add the water and combine by hand to form a rough ball. All flours are different, so you might need a little more water to form the ball. Let the pastry rest for 5 minutes in the fridge or at room temperature.

On a lightly floured bench, roll the pastry into a rectangle, about 20 × 50 cm (8 × 19½ in). Fold the top third of the pastry into the centre, then fold the bottom third up over that. Place the pastry back in the fridge and rest for 5 minutes. Repeat the rolling, folding and resting steps another three times – that's four in total. Finally, let the pastry rest in the fridge for another 20 minutes, or until you're ready to use it.

Preheat the oven to 180°C (350°F).

For the filling, heat a tablespoon of butter and oil in a flameproof casserole dish over a medium heat. Place the hare pieces in a bowl, season generously with salt and black pepper, then lightly dust with flour. Start to cook the hare in the dish. Once both sides are golden, remove the hare to a plate to rest.

Add the shallot, garlic, carrot, leek and celery to the dish and sauté for 2 minutes. Stir in the tomato purée and cook for a further minute, then add the wine, stock and herbs. Bring to the boil and add the hare.

Place the lid on, transfer to the oven and leave for 2 hours before checking. Once the meat is coming away from the bone, remove the hare and strain the sauce through a fine sieve.

Place the sauce back over a medium heat for about 15 minutes, to reduce down and thicken. Meanwhile, strip the hare meat off the bone, into a bowl, and place in the fridge.

Once the sauce has reduced to a thick gravy consistency, mix it through the hare meat. Roll the mixture into four balls about 5 cm (2 in) in diameter and place in the fridge to cool down. If you have any mixture left over, it is great tossed through pasta.

Roll out the pastry on a lightly floured bench, to a thickness of 3 mm (⅛ in). Using a 9 cm (3½ in) cutter, cut out eight discs of pastry, and place four on a roasting tin lined with baking paper. Pull the hare from the fridge and place a ball in the centre of each disc. Brush the egg wash around the edge of each pastry disc, then place the remaining four sheets on top, pressing down on the edges with a fork to seal, keeping the dome shape of the meat. Now, using the back of a small paring knife, score the pastry to decorate it, then brush with the rest of the egg wash.

Place in the oven and bake for about 8 minutes, or until golden brown. Let the pithiviers rest for 1 minute before serving with crisp vegetables or a fresh salad.

BRAISED RABBIT WITH MUSHROOMS, LENTILS & SPECK

I love one-pot cooking with rabbit. I have cooked this dish for the past twenty years and it has become a simpler dish with each incarnation – it started with a thick rich sauce, now it has a light broth stock. Cast-iron dishes are made for food like this; a camp cooker over a fire will work well, too.

SERVES 4

butter and oil, for cooking

1 rabbit, about 700 g (1 lb 9 oz),
    cut into sauté cuts

flour, for coating the rabbit

2 French shallots, sliced

2 garlic cloves, chopped

200 g (7 oz) field mushrooms, sliced

100 g (3½ oz) belly bacon
    (page 176), diced

1 bay leaf

1 thyme sprig

300 ml (10 fl oz) Game stock (page 210)
    or chicken stock

200 g (7 oz) green lentils

Preheat the oven to 160°C (320°F).

    Heat a tablespoon of butter and oil in a flameproof casserole dish over a medium heat. Place the rabbit pieces in a bowl and generously season with salt and black pepper, then lightly dust with flour.

    Start cooking the rabbit pieces in the dish. Once both sides are golden, remove to a plate to rest.

    Add the shallot, garlic, mushrooms, bacon and herbs to the casserole dish and cook over a medium heat for about 10 minutes, until the mushrooms start to lose their moisture and start to break down. Add the stock and bring to the boil. Stir the lentils into the boiling stock and place the rabbit pieces on top. Bring the liquid back up to a good boil and put the lid on.

    Transfer the dish to the oven and cook for 2 hours, or until the rabbit meat is coming away from the bone. Remove the dish from the oven and leave to rest for 15–20 minutes.

    Spoon the rabbit straight out of the dish to serve. Green beans or broccoli are a good match for this dish.

BONED ROLLED HARE

If you want to impress at your next dinner party, this is the dish for you. It looks complicated once done; just don't tell anyone how simple it is. And the filling is so versatile – once you get the technique down pat, you can use any meat you choose.

SERVES 8

caul fat (from deer, pig, sheep or goat, see page 10), for covering the hare, or 8–10 slices streaky bacon or prosciutto

1 boned-out hare, with the liver and heart

STUFFING

butter and oil, for cooking

1 brown onion, diced

1 garlic clove, crushed

100 g (3½ oz) field mushrooms, sliced

3 tablespoons fresh sourdough breadcrumbs

1 tablespoon chopped flat-leaf (Italian) parsley

a good pinch of ground mace

250 g (9 oz) minced (ground) pork

liver and heart of the hare, roughly chopped

sea salt flakes (1% of the overall weight of the stuffing mixture)

Preheat the oven to 180°C (350°F).

For the stuffing, heat a frying pan over a medium heat. Add about a tablespoon each of butter and oil, then fry the onion, garlic and mushrooms for 7 minutes, or until the liquid from the mushrooms dissipates.

Place the mixture in a food processor and pulse until chopped, but not puréed. Spread the mixture on a plate or tray, then cool in the fridge for 5 minutes.

Tip the mixture into a bowl. Add the breadcrumbs, parsley, mace, pork, and the hare liver and heart, mixing well.

Weigh the mixture, then add 1% of sea salt to the weight of the mixture. The mixture should weigh about 350 g (12½ oz), which means you'd need to add 3.5 g (1/12 oz) of salt. Season with ground black pepper. Mix thoroughly with a spatula or wooden spoon, then place the mixture back in the fridge.

Spread the caul fat or bacon slices out on a bench, making sure you leave enough space to overlap when rolling the hare. Place the hare on top and season with salt and pepper. Place the stuffing mixture lengthways down the centre of the hare, making a cylinder shape where the backbone was. Bring the sides of hare up over the mixture, to meet in the middle, so the stuffing is covered. Now take the caul fat edge closest to you and wrap it over the top, then roll away from you to make a cylinder. Tie the hare (see images on right), but not too tightly, or it will split when you seal it.

Heat a splash of oil in a roasting tin over a high heat, add the hare and seal for 30 seconds on each side, trying to cover as much of the roll as you can with a golden colour.

Place the roasting tin in the oven and roast the hare for 7 minutes, turning once.

Remove from the oven and let the hare rest for 7 minutes before you carve it.

The hare will be quite rare; if you prefer it more on the medium side, roast it for 10 minutes and rest for 10 minutes. I wouldn't roast it longer than 15 minutes, as it will dry out too much.

Serve with mash and wilted greens.

POSSUM ROGAN JOSH

Possum meat makes the best curries. I have done many different versions, but I find it takes well to the bold flavours of a rogan josh. I will guarantee that most people would think the meat has the same consistency of a free-range chicken thigh, tasting somewhere between rabbit and chicken – much like squirrel.

SERVES 4

1 onion, sliced

50 g (1¾ oz) ghee

4 green cardamom pods

6 cloves

2 bay leaves

2.5 cm (1 in) piece of cinnamon stick

2.5 cm (1 in) knob of fresh ginger, crushed

3 garlic cloves, crushed

450 g (1 lb) boned-out possum, cut into 2 cm (¾ in) cubes

1 teaspoon ground cumin

1 teaspoon chilli powder

2 teaspoons sweet paprika

1 teaspoon ground coriander

150 g (5½ oz) plain yoghurt

1 teaspoon salt

2 tablespoons chopped blanched almonds

1 tablespoon poppy seeds, ground

pinch of saffron threads, activated (see note on page 49)

Heat a heavy-based pot over a high heat. Fry the onion and ghee for about 5 minutes, until the onion is lightly browned. Add the cardamom pods, cloves, bay leaves and cinnamon and fry for a further minute. Stir in the ginger and garlic, then add the possum meat.

Sprinkle the cumin, chilli, paprika and coriander over the top and fry the mixture for 2 minutes. Add the yoghurt and salt. Cover and cook for 5–7 minutes, or until the sauce splits from dry to oily.

Remove the lid. Add the almonds and poppy seeds and fry for 1–2 minutes. Stir in 350 ml (12 fl oz) water, then cover and cook for 40–50 minutes, or until the meat is tender and the mixture is fairly dry.

Sprinkle with the saffron and cook gently for another 5 minutes, taking care the possum doesn't stick; rogan josh is a dry curry, with moist spices around the meat.

Serve with steamed rice and your favourite curry condiments; I like cucumber raita and tomato kachumber with this dish.

SLOW-ROASTED POSSUM LEG WITH GARLIC & ROSEMARY

I used to cook this at Zoe in London in the early 1990s, using chicken. It is based on a rustic Italian dish – one pan in the oven, then shared by the whole table. It's great with a side of salad or vegetables.

SERVES 2

4 possum legs

3 tablespoons olive oil, for cooking

3 medium-sized Dutch cream potatoes, washed, then sliced approximately 1 cm (½ in) thick

1–2 brown onions, sliced

3 garlic cloves, crushed

3 rosemary sprigs

250 ml (8½ fl oz/1 cup) Game stock (page 210) or chicken stock

Preheat the oven to 175°C (345°F).

Heat a heavy-based ovenproof frying pan or flameproof casserole dish over a high heat.

Place the possum legs in a bowl and season generously with salt and black pepper. Add a tablespoon of the olive oil to the pan, then sear the possum legs until golden brown all over. Remove and set aside.

Add another tablespoon of the oil to the pan and fry the potato slices for about 5 minutes, or until golden, then set aside with the possum.

Add the remaining oil to the pan and sauté the onion for about 10 minutes, until it becomes slightly translucent. Add the garlic, rosemary and stock and bring to the boil. Layer the potatoes in the pan and place the possum legs on top.

Place the whole pan or dish in the oven. Check after 25 minutes, adding a little more stock if the pan has gone dry.

After another 15 minutes in the oven, check to see if the legs are cooked by pressing on the meat; it should break away from the bone. If not, roast it a little longer, but don't overcook it or the meat will become dry.

Rest the possum for 10 minutes before serving.

ANIMAL DISEASES

When harvesting wild game, we are harvesting some of the finest and freshest meat on the planet, from animals that have been free to roam, with virtually no intervention in their growth in terms of their feed – all of which enhances the meat's quality and flavour. Still, one question at the back of many hunters' minds is, how safe is this meat from disease, whether natural or otherwise?

There are a few things to look out for that will give you confidence when harvesting animals, so you can be assured that you are doing it safely. Remember, though, that it is your responsibility to get to know the local environment where you are hunting. Find out if local rangers or any local authority is involved in controlling animal populations – some population control measures could include poisons or the introduction of disease.

When you do harvest an animal, look through the internal organs to see if there is any sign of disease, and check the carcass, when you are cutting it up, for cysts and abnormal signs in the flesh. In Australia, most parasites and disease are located in the organs, whereas America and Europe have meat-borne diseases such as CWD (chronic wasting disease) and parasites such as botfly. In Australia, we battle the flies once an animal is down, with blowflies being the main culprits that lay eggs on the meat if it's not bagged quick enough, resulting in maggots.

Below are a few diseases and problems that you can check for in Australia. When you get to know your local environment, you will have the information to cover your patch. These are just a few guidelines, as I don't pretend to be an expert on this subject.

In parts of Australia, 1080 poison is used for vermin control. It will leave an electric-blue tinge through the intestines of an animal and around the stomach. Do not eat anything from this animal – and if you can retrieve the carcass, please do so, as it will kill anything that eats it. Make sure you also wash everything that has been in contact with this carcass.

Worms in Australia include hydatid and taeniid tapeworms, as well as round, hook and whip worms. Worms are a parasite usually found in the offal of animals. They can be detected as a cyst on the flesh, presenting as a white lump, and internally they usually appear on the liver as white spots. If worms are found in the intestinal area or liver, then the meat is fine to eat, but don't eat the offal. However, if they are presenting as a cyst on the flesh, don't eat the meat at all. Some animals such as kangaroos and wallabies always have worms in their stomach, as these are part of their digestive system, and the meat is fine to harvest.

Toxoplasmosis is spread from feral cats to other animals. If it's in the area, the animals are usually in poor condition and low in body and muscle mass. This parasitic disease can also not show any signs, so be careful wherever there is a big feral cat population. If you shoot cats, try not to handle them at all. Don't eat any game that is infected with this parasite.

Myxomatosis and calicivirus are rabbit-borne diseases. The telltale signs in rabbits are puffy closed eyes as they eventually go blind and starve. If you see this, put the animal out of its misery and don't eat it.

Just remember, if you have harvested an animal that is in bad condition in terms of its body and muscle mass, take the time to check to see if there are any abnormal signs in the internal organs, or on the body itself – and get to know what parasites and diseases are found in your local hunting area, and what the animals are eating.

And always keep to the golden rule, 'When in doubt, chuck it out'.

PIG GOAT & CAMEL

Wild pigs or boars are both cherished and cursed all over the world. Their destruction in agriculture is second to none, but their meat is prized in Europe, America, Asia and the Antipodes. I find harvesting wild pigs quite strange, as I once farmed pigs for a living and would do farm kills for our own table. When you are in the field, you don't have the luxury of being able to scald them to remove the hair. Pigs also carry a lot of diseases, so you have to be careful when you harvest them, checking the internal organs, and also looking at the environment in which they are living with regard to the quality of their feed.

Goat is often claimed to be the most eaten meat in the world – incorrectly, as it turns out, because pork is. But goat is undoubtedly a tasty, versatile meat available in most places around the globe, with a healthy population in the wild as well. There is a big overseas market for Australian goat meat, with many being trapped in the outback and exported live.

Goats are part of the bovidae family, which also includes mountain goats, Himalayan tahr, chamois and bighorn sheep. New Zealand has a thriving population of tahr and chamois, bringing in an estimated $50 million a year from international hunting, with those species being at the top of the list. Europe has a massive chamois population, while America is known for its bighorn sheep and mountain goats.

Unfortunately, due to lockdowns during COVID in Australia, camel is one of the species I never got to hunt. I have cooked a fair bit of camel meat though, and the recipes I have put together have been tried and tested. Camels were brought to Australia by British settlers via India, Afghanistan and the Middle East. Due to the environment of outback Australia, the camels flourished and became a major problem for the agriculture sector, with damage to fences, feed and crops. In 2007, they were listed as a feral species, meaning they can be hunted without a cull license and there is no hunting season. By 2008, the camel population had grown to around 1 million and by 2009, the government had implemented a $19 million plan to reduce the numbers. The population was down to 300,000 by the end of that year. In Australia, camel meat is harvested and shipped all over the world for human consumption. Places like the Middle East, Africa, Europe and Asia are big fans of the meat. Camel meat is low in cholesterol and high in protein like most game meats, and we should be eating more of it.

PIG

LIST OF CUTS

1 Neck scotch (collar/butt)
roasting
grilling
braising

2 Hocks
braising

3 Shoulder
slow-roasting
mincing for sausages

4 Belly
braising
twice-cooking
roasting, grilling

5 Loin
roasting
grilling
curing

6 Eye fillets
grilling
roasting

7 Leg
roasting
slow cooking
curing

8 Round
curing

9 Ribs
barbecuing
grilling
braising

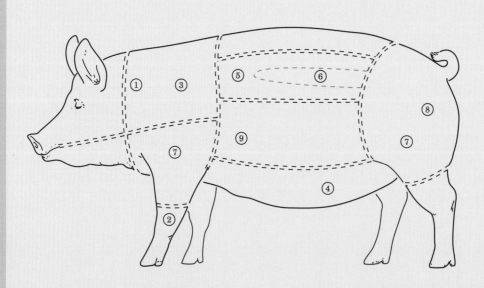

GOAT / TAHR / CHAMOIS / BIGHORN / SHEEP

LIST OF CUTS

1 Neck chops
braising

2 Loin chops
grilling

3 Backstraps
roasting
grilling

4 Shoulder
roasting
mincing (grinding)

5 Legs
roasting
braising

6 Shanks
braising

7 Ribs
grilling
twice-cooking

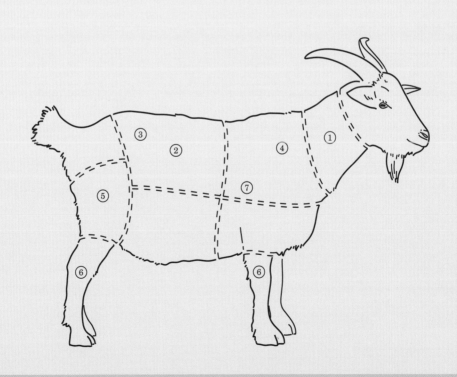

CAMEL

LIST OF CUTS

1 **Neck chops**
braising

2 **Loin chops**
grilling

3 **Backstraps**
roasting
grilling

4 **Shoulder**
roasting
mincing (grinding)

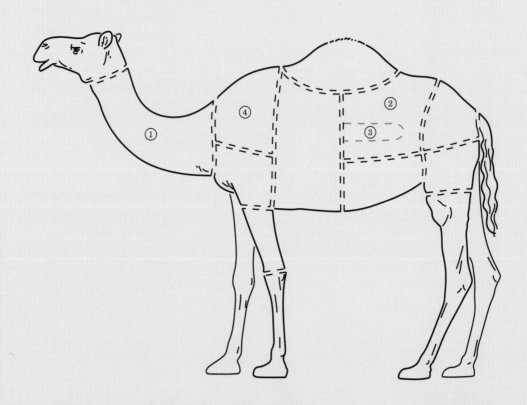

NOT NICK'S PORK & CHIVE POT STICKERS

I've got this mate who stole my recipe for his cheese book, changed a thing or two and rubbed it in that my recipe was his now. Well, it's coming right back at ya now, Haddow! I'm changing one thing – but I'm not as lazy as you, Haddow, as I make my own dumpling wrappers.

MAKES 20

vegetable oil, for frying

Chinese black vinegar, to serve

DUMPLING DOUGH

320 g (11½ oz) plain (all-purpose) flour

175 ml (6 fl oz) warm water, at 45°C (115°F)

FILLING

500 g (1 lb 2 oz) minced (ground) pork

1 thumb-sized knob of fresh ginger, peeled and finely grated

1 spring onion (scallion), finely diced

1 garlic clove, crushed

2 tablespoons finely chopped chives

3 teaspoons fish sauce

2 teaspoons sesame oil

30 ml (1 fl oz) soy sauce

Preheat the oven to 120°C (250°F).

To make the dough, place the flour in a mixing bowl and slowly start to add the water while mixing (you can do this by hand, or using an electric mixer). Continue until it starts to form a ball; this should take about a minute. Remove from the bowl and continue to knead on a lightly floured bench until it forms a nice smooth ball. Place the ball back into the bowl, cover with a damp towel and leave to rest for a minimum of 30 minutes; the dough can be made the day before and left overnight in the fridge.

In a bowl, mix together all the filling ingredients.

Take your rested dough and roll it into one long cylinder, about 2.5 cm (1 in) in diameter, then cut into portions. (I find with this size of dough you can get about 25 portions, so you have a few spare. You can never have enough dumplings!) Make sure you place them back under the damp towel after you cut them, as they dry out quickly. And do them one at a time, to make sure the pastry doesn't dry out and crack.

Cut the dough in half, roll each half into a cylinder, then cut 10 even pieces from each cylinder, to give 20 pieces.

My kitchen hack for rolling the dough pieces out is simple – I take a portion of the dough and press it using a tortilla press, ready for filling. If you don't have a tortilla press, just roll the dough pieces into a circle with a rolling pin, about 2–3 mm (⅛–⅙ in) thick.

To shape the dumplings, place a heaped tablespoon of the pork mixture in the middle of a wrapper, brush to the edges with a pastry brush moistened with water and bring the edges together, pinching to seal. Repeat until the filling or the pastry is finished.

It's best to do this no more than an hour before your cooking time. If left too long, the filling can leak into the pastry and spoil the dumplings. If you are preparing them before your feasting day, place the dumplings in the freezer and cook from frozen.

To cook the dumplings, heat a tablespoon of vegetable oil in a frying pan with a tight-fitting lid over a medium heat. When hot, add as many dumplings as will fit in the pan, without overcrowding. Cook without moving the dumplings for 1 minute, then add 80 ml (2½ fl oz/⅓ cup) water and cover with a lid. When the water has evaporated, the dumplings should be cooked through and have a golden crisp bottom.

Repeat in batches, keeping the cooked dumplings warm in the oven.

Serve the dumplings warm, with Chinese black vinegar as a dipping sauce.

‡ **NOTE**
If you are as lazy as Nick, instead of making your
own dumpling dough you can just purchase a packet
of gow gee wrappers from a supermarket.

PORK LOIN SALTIMBOCCA

Saltimbocca translates to 'it jumps in the mouth'. This Italian dish is made with all different types of meat, from veal to chicken and even pork. The saltimbocca part is always the same: wrapped in prosciutto, with fresh sage leaves. This version is a wonderful combination: pork on pork with fresh herbs. It's an easy one-pan dish that matches with just about any type of side dish you can imagine.

SERVES 4

8 trimmed pork loin steaks,
     each 2 cm (¾ in) thick
8 prosciutto slices
8 sage leaves
olive oil and butter, for cooking

Give the pork loin steaks a little thumping with a meat mallet, until they are about 1 cm (½ in) thick. (If you don't have a meat mallet, a bottle or rolling pin will do fine.)

Lay the eight prosciutto slices on a clean surface, with space in between, and place a sage leaf on each. Give a good grinding of black pepper, then lay a pork steak on each. Bring one side of the prosciutto up and over the pork, then tuck it in underneath the loin. Now pick up the pork loin, wrap the other prosciutto side over, then tuck that one in as well.

Heat a frying pan over a high heat and add some oil. Once the pan is hot, add the wrapped loin steaks and cook for 3 minutes on one side, making sure when you turn that they are golden brown underneath. Continue to cook for a further 3 minutes.

Add a knob of butter and swirl in the pan until it dissolves. Add fresh cracked black pepper and serve.

‡ NOTE
The prosciutto slices should be big enough to wrap quite comfortably over and around the flattened pork loin steaks. If you wanted to do a mini version of these, I would recommend using a toothpick to hold everything in place, but for this large version there is no need.

COCHINITA PIBIL

Cochinita pibil is a traditional Mexican suckling pig dish from the Yucatán Peninsula. I know it as *puerco pibil*, a version made with pork butt, from the Robert Rodriguez film *Once Upon a Time in Mexico*, and after watching that movie, I just had to make this dish! It's very versatile – you can eat the pulled pork in rolls, tacos, or with rice and beans. One of the main ingredients is annatto seeds, which give the dish its burnt-red orange colour.

MAKES 2 KG (4 LB 6 OZ)

3 kg (6 lb 10 oz) pork scotch fillet
30 g (1 oz) annatto seeds
30 g (1 oz) cumin seeds
30 g (1 oz) coriander seeds
10 g (¼ oz) whole cloves
10 g (¼ oz) black peppercorns
30 g (1 oz) sweet paprika
150 ml (5 fl oz) orange juice
50 ml (1¾ fl oz) lemon juice
100 ml (3½ fl oz) white wine vinegar
8 garlic cloves, crushed
1 red onion, roughly chopped
30 g (1 oz) salt
banana leaves, for wrapping

Preheat the oven to 160°C (320°F).

Dice the pork into 5 cm (2 in) cubes and place in a bowl.

Place all the whole spices in a frying pan and lightly toast them over a medium heat for a few minutes, until fragrant, then grind to a fine powder. Add to a blender with the paprika, orange and lemon juice, vinegar, garlic, onion and salt and blend for up to a minute, until smooth.

Pour the liquid over the pork and mix through. Cover the pork and place in the fridge overnight.

The next day, line a baking dish with banana leaves and pour the pork mixture on top. Cover the pork with more leaves, then encase the pork in the leaves, using either string or foil.

Place the dish in the oven and cook for 4 hours. When the pork is cooked, it will just pull apart and is ready to use.

‡ NOTE
You'll need to start this dish the day before.

SCOTCH EGGS

I love a good Scotch egg. I have mixed it up a bit here by adding venison and tossing in some panko breadcrumbs. The ultimate dish for 'pocket food dining'.

MAKES 8

10 free-range eggs

300 g (10½ oz) minced (ground) pork

200 g (7 oz) minced (ground) venison

30 g (1 oz) Mustard (page 200)

30 g (1 oz/⅔ cup) chopped chives

1 thyme sprig, chopped

300 g (10½ oz/2 cups) plain
   (all-purpose) flour

100 g (3½ oz/1¼ cups)
   fresh breadcrumbs

100 g (3½ oz/1⅔ cups)
   panko breadcrumbs

60 ml (2 fl oz) milk

rice bran oil, for deep-frying

Place eight of the eggs in a pan of cold water, bring to the boil, then simmer over a medium heat for 2 minutes. Remove the eggs, refresh in a bowl of iced water and set aside.

Mix the pork, venison, mustard and herbs in a bowl and season with salt and pepper. Form the mixture into eight patties.

Carefully peel the eggs and gently pat dry. Enclose each egg in a patty, shaping with your hands to ensure the egg is completely covered with the meat. Place the balls in the fridge for 20 minutes.

Season the flour with salt and pepper, then spread on a plate. Mix and spread out all the breadcrumbs on a separate plate.

In a bowl, beat the milk with the remaining two eggs.

Roll the encased eggs first in the flour, then in the milk mixture, and finally in the breadcrumbs to coat well. Place back in the fridge for 20 minutes.

Half-fill a deep-fryer or a large heavy-based pan with rice bran oil and heat to 170°C (340°F). Fry the Scotch eggs in batches for around 7 minutes, until the coating is golden brown. Let the eggs rest for 1 minute.

Serve the eggs warm or cold, with a good dash of hot sauce.

GOAT RENDANG

One of my fondest memories from living and working in West Sumatra, Indonesia, for three years is of all the great restaurants serving 'nasi padang' – a kind of banquet where you choose from an array of famously hot and spicy ready-to-eat dishes that are displayed in the front window, and they bring your selection to your table with a good serving of steamed rice. One of the best-known nasi padang dishes is rendang, a spicy slow-cooked stew made with meat – most commonly beef and beef heart. My friend's mum used to make us a rendang from jackfruit, and we would have to let her know when we were coming to the village, as it was cooked over an open fire and took two days to make. Goat also lends itself to this curry really well. This version doesn't take two days to make – but as with all curries, the flavour gets better if made a day ahead.

SERVES 8

100 g (3½ oz/1⅔ cups) shredded coconut (fresh coconut if you can get it, otherwise dried is fine)

50 g (1¾ oz) fresh ginger, peeled and roughly chopped

50 g (1¾ oz) turmeric (fresh is best, but you can also use dried)

4 garlic cloves, peeled and roughly chopped

6 red chillies, topped and roughly chopped

4 candlenuts

2 kg (4 lb 6 oz) goat leg or shoulder, diced

400 ml (13½ fl oz) tin coconut cream

50 ml (1¾ fl oz) rice bran oil

lemon juice, to taste

Toast the coconut in a frying pan over a medium heat for 2 minutes, or until golden brown.

Place the coconut in a food processor with the ginger, turmeric, garlic, chillies and candlenuts and blitz to a fine paste. (If you have time to pound the ingredients together using a mortar and pestle, you will get a better-tasting curry, as a mortar and pestle extract the oils and flavour better from bruising all the spices, whereas a food processor shreds and shears the ingredients, and doesn't extract the aromatics quite as well.)

Place the goat meat in a bowl, mix in the paste and coconut cream and leave to sit for 20 minutes.

Heat a lidded pot over a medium heat. Add the oil, then the meat. Bring the curry up to a steady simmer, stirring constantly to ensure the mixture doesn't stick.

Turn the curry down to a slow simmer and place the lid on. This will help to quicken the cooking process and also keep moisture in the pot, to stop the curry sticking. Cook for 2–3 hours, checking and stirring now and then to make sure it's not sticking to the bottom.

Remove the lid. Turn the heat back up to medium. Stand over the pot and cook the sauce down for about 10–15 minutes, stirring to make sure it doesn't stick. You want this curry to reduce right down and be a dry curry, with moist spices around the meat.

Once the sauce has cooked down, season with lemon juice, salt and pepper. Serve with rice and your favourite curry condiments.

MIDDLE EASTERN SPICED GOAT LEG

Most people love to cook lamb with Middle Eastern spices. I also find goat stands up to these spices very well. The spices here can be substituted with a baharat spice mix, if you don't feel like putting your own together. This is a great summer dish to have with salad.

SERVES 8

1 goat leg

60 g (2 oz) ground black pepper

30 g (1 oz) ground coriander

30 g (1 oz) ground cinnamon

30 g (1 oz) ground cloves

40 g (1½ oz) ground cumin

20 g (¾ oz) ground mace

10 g (¼ oz) ground cardamom

60 g (2 oz) sweet paprika

3 brown onions, sliced

lemon juice, to taste

Preheat the oven to 150°C (300°F).

Place the goat leg in a bowl with all the spices and give them all a good rubbing into the meat.

Place the onion in a roasting tin, pour in about 250 ml (8½ fl oz/1 cup) water, put the meat on top and then into the oven. Check the leg every hour to see whether or not it is too coloured and needs covering with foil to stop it burning. It should take around 4–5 hours before the meat starts to fall off the bone.

As with all meat, let it rest for 10 minutes once it comes out of the oven. Give it a squeeze of lemon before you serve. This is great with pilaf rice.

GRILLED BARNSLEY GOAT CHOPS WITH ROASTED TOMATO SALSA

At one of the restaurants I worked for in London, we had our own butchery, and it was also the first time I ever worked with wild game. The head chef, Konrad Melling, was a northerner who grew up around game and had an exceptional knowledge about it, as well as a great knowledge of animal cuts. We used to run a 'Barnsley chop' on the menu, and I have never forgotten it. Made famous by the Brooklands Hotel in Barnsley, it was cut from the mid-section of a lamb loin, straight across the loin, about 2.5 cm (1 in) thick, to give you two chops. I know, how good's that? I love goat chops – and what better than to have two of them.

SERVES 4

4 Barnsley goat chops
rice bran oil, for grilling

ROASTED TOMATO SALSA
6 tomatoes, seeded and halved
olive oil, for cooking
1 red onion, diced
3 red chillies, chopped
3 garlic cloves, crushed
juice of 1 lemon
20 g (¾ oz) coriander (cilantro) leaves, chopped

Preheat the oven to 200°C (400°F).

To make the salsa, place the tomato halves in a roasting tin, cut side down, and brush with olive oil. Bake for 15 minutes, or until the tops are golden.

While the tomatoes are cooking, slowly sweat (cook without colour) the onion, chilli and garlic in a frying pan over a low heat for about 10 minutes.

Once done, place the tomatoes and onion mixture in a food processor. Add the lemon juice, season with salt and pepper and process until smooth.

Remove from the food processor and fold the coriander through. Set aside at room temperature.

Heat whatever implement you are cooking the chops on to high. (I prefer to cook over charcoal, so my fire has burnt down to the charcoal cooking stage before I start; this can take 30–40 minutes, depending on the wood used.)

Brush your chops with rice bran oil and season both sides with salt and pepper. Don't be shy with the seasoning – I like to use good-quality sea salt flakes and freshly ground black pepper.

Place the chops on your cooking surface and grill for a couple of minutes, until you have a good brown colour underneath, then turn and do the other side. This should take about 3–4 minutes each side.

Remove the chops from the heat and keep them in a warm place to rest for 10 minutes before serving. The resting time will help the meat relax, and also continue to cook the meat closer to the bone.

Once the chops are plated, top with the salsa and serve with green leaves, or a crisp green such as lightly steamed asparagus or beans.

GOAT SHOULDER WITH DRY RUB, LEMON & ANCHOVY

1 goat shoulder
1 lemon, sliced
30 g (1 oz) Dry rub (page 209)
5 anchovy fillets

This is the dish that enticed a vegetarian of seventeen years' standing to start eating meat again. Mind you, Emma (my wife) was breastfeeding twins at the time. I used to cook it in our wood-fired combustion stove over a few hours – and I've also twice-cooked the shoulder by sealing it in a food vacuum bag, simmering the bag in water for 3–4 hours, then removing the goat from the bag and crisping it up on a barbecue. As with most things, there is more than one way to get the same result.

SERVES 8

Preheat the oven to 150°C (300°F).

Place the goat shoulder in a bowl with all the ingredients and give them all a good rubbing into the meat.

Now place the meat in a roasting tin, pour about 250 ml (8½ fl oz/1 cup) water into the bottom and place it in the oven. Check the shoulder every hour to see whether or not it is too coloured and needs covering with foil to stop it burning. It should take around 4–5 hours before the meat starts to fall off the bone.

As with all meat, let it rest for 10 minutes before serving. It's great with anything from salads to greens and vegetables, and even on flatbread kebabs.

GAME MIXED GRILL WITH CHAMP & BRAISED FIELD MUSHROOMS

When I was travelling around Australia by car, I made it my mission to eat the mixed grill at every pub I visited. The Australian mixed grill is very docile compared to the offal-loaded mixed grills of Britain. Mine is a good mixture of both, but you can't go past champ and mushrooms as a side.

SERVES 2

4 slices of belly bacon (page 176)

2 fillet steaks (of whatever game you like)

2 goat's kidneys, split top to bottom and threaded onto skewers

2 × ½ cm (¼ in) slices pig's liver

2 slices deer's heart

1 Hunter's sausage (page 188), split lengthways

GARNISH

4 field mushrooms

2 garlic cloves, crushed

1 rosemary sprig

1 thyme sprig

20 g (¾ oz) butter

olive oil, for drizzling

CHAMP

300 g (10½ oz) king edward potatoes, or any good mashing spud, peeled and sliced

30 g (1 oz) unsalted butter

50 ml (1¾ fl oz) thick (double/heavy) cream

3 spring onions (scallions), chopped

Preheat the oven to 170°C (340°F).

To make the garnish, get a roasting tin and place the mushrooms in it, stalk side up. Add the garlic, herbs and butter, then season with salt and pepper. Splash a little oil around, cover with foil and place in the oven. Bake for 1–2 hours, until the mushrooms have lost their moisture. Leave the roasting tin out at room temperature to cool down.

Meanwhile, get started on the champ. Place the potatoes in a saucepan and cover with water. Bring to the boil, then turn the heat down to a steady simmer and cook for 15–20 minutes. Check the potatoes by piercing them with the tip of a paring knife; if they slide off easily, they are ready. Drain the potatoes and set aside.

Return the drained pot to a medium heat with the butter and cream. Cook until the butter has melted, then remove from the heat.

Pass the potatoes through a potato ricer, mouli or food mill, into the melted cream and butter. Place back on the heat and cook, stirring, until fully combined. Fold the spring onion through and season with salt and pepper. Keep the champ warm.

Grill all the meat items and make sure to season them all, except the bacon and sausage. Once they are cooked to your liking, arrange on a plate with a couple of mushrooms and a good scoop of champ.

CAMEL & GREEN OLIVE TAGINE

I first made this tagine with a good friend, Kurt Sampson, who I worked with in London and then reunited with twenty years later in a kitchen in Melbourne. I hadn't done much, if any, Middle Eastern cooking, but Kurt had been enmeshed in it for the previous fifteen years. He told me this is the go-to tagine; I think the camel meat is a perfect fit.

SERVES 6

1 kg (2 lb 3 oz) diced camel topside

2 brown onions, 1 chopped, 1 sliced

4 tomatoes, 2 chopped, 2 sliced

2 large Dutch cream potatoes, or other creamy-fleshed spuds, scrubbed well and cut into wedges; I like the skin left on

150 g (5½ oz) green olives, pitted

½ bunch of coriander (cilantro), chopped

MARINADE

2 garlic cloves, roughly chopped

1 thumb-sized knob of fresh ginger, roughly chopped

1–2 preserved lemons, rind only, roughly chopped

2 brown onions, roughly chopped

1 red chilli

1 tablespoon sweet paprika

1 tablespoon ground cumin

2 tablespoons chopped coriander (cilantro)

2 tablespoons chopped flat-leaf (Italian) parsley

1–2 teaspoons saffron threads, activated (see note on page 49)

125 ml (4 fl oz/½ cup) olive oil

2 bay leaves

Combine all the marinade ingredients except the bay leaves in a food processor and blend until thoroughly combined, then add the whole bay leaves.

Place the camel in a bowl and mix in half the marinade. Cover and refrigerate for at least 2 hours, or overnight.

Combine the chopped onion and tomato and spread over the base of a tagine dish. Place the camel pieces in the centre of the tagine. Top the camel with the potato wedges and the sliced tomato and onions, then spread the rest of the marinade on top. Stick the olives around in any gaps. Top with the coriander and 250 ml (8½ fl oz/1 cup) water.

Cover the tagine with the lid and cook over a very low heat on the stove for 2 hours. You must leave the lid on the whole time and not stir the tagine. (You could also cook it in an oven set at 130°C/265°F for 3 hours if you wish.)

I like to serve my tagine with a tomato and onion salad and bitter green leaves.

‡ NOTE

If you don't have a traditional earthenware tagine, a flameproof casserole dish with a lid will do just fine.

87

SHREDDED CAMEL IN GAME BROTH WITH POTATO DUMPLINGS

This dish is a homage to my late grandmother, Mary Magdalen Staniforth, a.k.a. Molly. It reminds me of her style of slow cooking, and the suet dumplings she used to make, which were off-the-charts delicious. I have put my own twist on the dish with the potato dumplings, and I find camel shoulder is the best cut. This is a great base recipe, and the list of what you can add to customise it to your taste is pretty much endless.

SERVES 4

500 g (1 lb 2 oz) boneless camel shoulder

3 French shallots, thinly sliced

2 garlic cloves, thinly sliced

2 litres (68 fl oz/8 cups) Game stock (page 210)

2 handfuls of flat-leaf (Italian) parsley, chopped

POTATO DUMPLINGS

500 g (1 lb 2 oz) king edward, Dutch cream or other floury potatoes, peeled

100 g (3½ oz/⅔ cup) plain (all-purpose) flour

1 free-range egg, whisked

½ bunch of chives, finely chopped

a pinch of ground nutmeg

Place the camel, shallot and garlic in a stockpot. Pour in the stock and bring to the boil over a high heat. Turn the heat down to a slow simmer and cook for 3–4 hours, or until the camel meat falls apart. At this stage, just turn the heat off and leave the meat in the stock. This would also work in a slow cooker.

To make the dumplings, cook the potatoes in a saucepan of salted boiling water. Drain well, then pass through a potato ricer, mouli or food mill, into a bowl. Set aside to cool for 20 minutes.

By hand, combine the cooled potato with the flour, egg, chives and nutmeg; if you don't like getting your hands dirty, use a wooden or plastic spoon. You don't want to overmix the dough, or the dumplings won't be fluffy. Season with salt and pepper. Roll one-quarter of the potato mixture at a time into a long cylinder with a diameter of about 3 cm (1¼ in). Make a cut every 1.5 cm (½ in) and roll into balls.

Remove the camel meat from the stock and break it apart amongst your serving bowls, then sprinkle with the parsley.

Bring the stock back up to the boil, add the dumplings, then turn the heat down to a rolling simmer. Cook the dumplings until they float to the top, which should take no longer than 3 minutes.

Spread the dumplings evenly among the bowls and top with the hot stock.

CHERMOULA CAMEL KOFTAS WITH FALAFELS & TAHINI YOGHURT

Here's a great little mezze plate. And yes, I'm not all about meat – I used to make a fresh falafel mix to sell at my market stall to break up the overload of pork, which I was raising and processing. My secret is using both broad beans and chickpeas in the falafel mix. You'll need to soak them overnight, so start a day ahead.

SERVES 6

KOFTAS

500 g (1 lb 2 oz) minced (ground) camel

1 brown onion, grated

2 garlic cloves, crushed

1 teaspoon ground cumin

1 teaspoon ground coriander

1 teaspoon ground allspice

1 teaspoon ground black pepper

2 teaspoons sea salt flakes

¼ bunch of flat-leaf (Italian) parsley, chopped

20 ml (¾ fl oz) vegetable oil

FALAFELS

300 g (10½ oz) dried broad (fava) beans, soaked for 24 hours, then peeled

200 g (7 oz) dried chickpeas, soaked for 24 hours

3 spring onions (scallions), roughly chopped

3 garlic cloves, peeled

1 bunch of coriander (cilantro), roughly chopped

1 teaspoon cumin, ground

a good pinch of bicarbonate of soda (baking soda)

oil, for deep-frying

TAHINI YOGHURT

200 g (7 oz) plain yoghurt

1 garlic clove, crushed

2 tablespoons tahini

lemon juice, salt and pepper to taste

To make the koftas, combine the camel, onion, garlic, spices, pepper, salt and parsley in a large bowl. Using a wooden spoon or your hand, fold the oil through to help bind the mixture. Divide the mixture into six balls, then shape them into cylinders using the palm of your hand.

To make the falafels, place all the ingredients, except the oil, in a food processor and blend until they form a paste. Roll the mixture into 12 balls, then press down on each ball to make a little oval shape.

Combine all the tahini yoghurt ingredients in a bowl and set aside.

To cook the koftas, I find the best way is over coals. It produces the best flavour and takes the dish to the next level, but you can also cook these in a frying pan for about 3 minutes on each side. The falafels can be deep-fried or shallow-fried in the oil until golden brown.

To serve this dish, place all the elements on a platter and serve with flatbreads.

Fire cooking

N.04

WALLABY
& KANGAROO

Wallaby and kangaroo are indigenous to Australia, and part of our incredible range of unique native wildlife. We have massive numbers of kangaroos across many regions of mainland Australia, as well as a large population of wallabies in Tasmania.

When I lived on Bruny Island – an island off southern Tasmania – I held a game harvester's licence for wallaby for eight years, and was lucky enough to have a game abattoir on the island, owned and operated by Richard Clark, a real character. To this day, I haven't seen anyone who can match his skinning and cutting skills.

Eating an iconic Australia animal doesn't resonate with many, but maybe if they knew that our estimated 50 million kangaroos could be selectively harvested by professionals, I believe more people would see them as a great free-range, organic, grass-fed, sustainable source of protein.

Selective harvesting is a form of conservation. When an animal population becomes too large for an area, it impacts the environment, as well as the animals' welfare. Managed well, within a balanced ecosystem, these healthy wild kangaroo populations can become a sustainable source of protein for generations to come.

Too many animals in Australia are shot for culling purposes, then left to rot, unutilised. America and Europe have embedded hunting as a consumable resource in their way of life, and I believe Australia should follow.

WALLABY / KANGAROO

LIST OF CUTS

1 Tail
braising

2 Backstraps
grilling

3 Topside
grilling

4 Forequarters
smoking low 'n' slow, braising

5 Haunch
twice-cooking
roasting
braising

6 Shanks
braising

Skinning a kangaroo tail

KANGAROO-TAIL SAUSAGE ROLLS

There are two camps in this world: pie or sausage roll. I'm in the sausage roll one, for sure. Sausage rolls are very unassuming when it comes to what you can put inside them – I hide tonnes of veg in the ones I make for the kids at home. This is a recipe from an event dinner I did with Canadian chef André Daoust. Before I could get to make these on the day, André had smashed out the filling mixture, and we even deep-fried the rolls before baking them. They were incredible: the pastry fluffed up and the filling was on point. The tailbone gives a rich gelatinous flavour and glossy shine, and it sets in a similar way as oxtail does when cooked.

MAKES 12 LUNCH-SIZE ROLLS

oil and butter, for cooking and
    deep-frying
1 kangaroo tail, cut into 6 portions
3 French shallots, sliced
5 garlic cloves, crushed
1 leek, white part only, chopped
200 ml (7 fl oz) Game stock (page 210)
1 tablespoon Mustard (page 200)

PASTRY
250 g (9 oz/1⅔ cups) bakers flour
a good pinch of salt
250 g (9 oz) unsalted butter
100 ml (3½ fl oz) cold water
1 egg, lightly beaten, for brushing

Preheat the oven to 180°C (350°F).

Place a lidded, ovenproof heavy-based saucepan with some oil over a high heat. Season the kangaroo tail pieces well with salt and pepper, then seal on both sides until golden brown. Remove the tail pieces and set aside.

Add some butter to the pan and cook off the shallot, garlic and leek for 2–3 minutes, or until slightly translucent. Add the stock and tail pieces and bring to the boil. Once the liquid is boiling, put the lid on.

Place the pan into the oven and cook for 3–4 hours, or until the meat falls off the bone. Remove from the oven, pick the meat out of the liquid and reserve.

Blend the liquid with a hand-held stick blender, then place it back over a medium heat for about 20–30 minutes, to reduce down by half. Stir in the mustard.

Pick all the meat away from the bone. Add some of the reduced stock to the meat to make it moist and sticky. (If you have any stock left over, use it in other dishes, or just as a straight-up gravy over a grilled piece of meat.) Once the meat mixture is done, check the seasoning and leave it to the side to cool down.

To make the pastry, sift the flour and salt into a large bowl. Add the butter and rub in using your fingers. Don't overdo it – you still want to see chunks of butter. Make a well in the centre, add the water and combine by hand to form a rough ball. (All flours are different, so you might need a little more water to form the ball.)

Let the pastry rest for 5 minutes. Then, on a lightly floured bench, roll it into a rectangle, about 20 × 50 cm (8 × 19½ in). Fold the top third of the pastry into the centre, then fold the bottom third up over that. Place it back in the fridge to rest for 5 minutes.

Repeat the steps (rolling, folding, resting) another three times – that's four in total. Then let the pastry rest in the fridge for a final 20 minutes before you use it. (This pastry can be made the day before.)

When you're ready to make the rolls, heat the oven to 180°C (350°F) and line a large baking tray with baking paper.

Cut the chilled pastry into four even portions. Roll out one of the pieces into a rectangle about 3 mm (⅛ in) thick. Using a tablespoon, spoon the meat mixture lengthways down the middle of the pastry rectangle, then lightly brush the pastry edges with egg wash. Take up the closest pastry edge and roll it over, forming a cylinder. Cut into three pieces, brush with more egg wash and place on the lined baking tray. Repeat with the remaining pastry and filling.

In a deep-fryer or heavy-based saucepan, heat 2 cm (¾ in) of oil to 170°C (340°F). Once hot, place some sausage rolls in the oil, making sure not to overcrowd the oil. Cook for 1–2 minutes to puff up the pastry, then place them back on the baking tray.

Bake the rolls in the oven for a further 5–7 minutes, until they are golden brown – remember, the filling is already cooked, so you are only cooking the pastry.

Let the rolls sit for 5 minutes, before serving with a home-made sauce. I like mustard (page 200) or a hot sauce with my sausage rolls, but barbecue or tomato sauce (page 205) are winners for most people.

‡ NOTE
The pastry can be made the day before.

1 wallaby haunch

1 brown onion, quartered

2 garlic cloves, crushed

5 juniper berries, crushed

2 bay leaves

100 ml (3½ fl oz) malt vinegar

2 tablespoons salt

3 tablespoons soft brown sugar

CORNING BRINE

200 g (7 oz) cooking sea salt

150 g (5½ oz) soft brown sugar

3 garlic cloves, crushed

1 tablespoon brown mustard seeds

1 tablespoon ground allspice

1 tablespoon ground mace

COLCANNON

1 kg (2 lb 3 oz) king edward potatoes, or other mashing potatoes, peeled and quartered

100 g (3½ oz) cultured butter

1 leek, white part only, chopped

2 kale leaves, chopped (or ¼ savoy cabbage)

2 tablespoons chopped chives

150 ml (5 fl oz) thickened (whipping) cream

CORNED HINDQUARTER OF WALLABY WITH COLCANNON

Corned meat and mash is a match made in heaven – and what's even better than corned meat and mash is corned meat and colcannon! Wallaby is a sweet meat that lends itself to corning incredibly well, and any leftovers are also great in a potato hash.

SERVES 6

Combine all the brine ingredients in a large pot. Add 2 litres (68 fl oz/8 cups) water and bring up to the boil. Once the salt and sugar have dissolved, remove from the heat and allow to cool down.

Place the wallaby in a clean bucket and cover with the cold brine. Place a plate or weight of some kind on top, to keep the wallaby fully submerged. Refrigerate for 3 days.

To cook the wallaby, place the haunch in a pot big enough to keep the whole haunch submerged. Add the onion, garlic, juniper berries, bay leaves, vinegar salt and sugar, and enough water to cover the haunch. Bring the liquid to the boil, then reduce to a slow simmer and cook for 2 hours, or until the meat comes away from the bone.

Remove from the heat and let the meat rest in the cooking liquor while you're preparing the colcannon.

To make the colcannon, add the potatoes to a pot of water with a good pinch of salt. Bring to the boil, then reduce to a rolling simmer and cook for about 15 minutes. Check the potatoes by poking a small knife into a cube and lifting it out – if the potato slides off, it is cooked. Once cooked, drain into a colander and set aside.

Add half the butter to the pot over a medium heat. Sweat down the leek and kale for 3–4 minutes, or until the leek is translucent. Now add the potatoes and beat them in using a wooden spoon. Add the chives, cream and remaining butter and continue to mix with your wooden spoon. Check the seasoning.

To serve, place the colcannon on a large carving tray, then remove the wallaby from the liquor and place on top. Give a good grinding of fresh black pepper over the top, carve the meat and serve.

CRISPY WALLABY SHANKS WITH HORSERADISH & PARSLEY SAUCE

Wallaby shanks are about the same size as chicken drumsticks. I have served them many times at events because they make a great finger food – and the meat has a fantastic texture when it's cooked right. This dish doesn't have to be a finger-food dish, though. It will go well with any game meat shanks you care to cook.

SERVES 2

4 wallaby shanks

200 ml (7 fl oz) Game stock (page 210)

2 garlic cloves, crushed

1 French shallot, sliced

70 g (2½ oz) cultured butter

2 tablespoons plain (all-purpose) flour

3 tablespoons Preserved horseradish (page 207)

1 bunch of flat-leaf (Italian) parsley, chopped

oil, for cooking

Place the shanks in a pot deep enough to cover them with the stock. Pour in the stock, add the garlic and shallot and bring to the boil, then reduce to a rolling simmer and cook for 15–20 minutes, or until the meat starts to get soft, but is not falling off the bone.

Remove the shanks from the stock and set aside. Pour the stock into a jug and set aside.

Melt the butter in the pot over a medium heat, then stir in the flour and let it cook out for 1–2 minutes. Slowly start to add the stock to the roux, stirring constantly so lumps don't form. Once all the stock is added, bring to the boil, then reduce to a rolling simmer and cook for a further 3 minutes, stirring all the while, as you don't want the shallot sticking to the bottom.

Add the horseradish and parsley and cook for a further minute. Check the seasoning and set aside.

Warm up a frying pan, griddle or chargrill pan to a high heat. Give your wallaby shanks a good coating of oil and season generously with salt and pepper. Make sure you do season them well, as poached meat needs a lot of seasoning to bring the flavour back out with the crispy crust.

Add the shanks to the hot pan and cook until golden brown on all sides; this should only take 5–10 minutes, maximum.

Once the shanks are done, place them on your serving plates and top with the horseradish sauce.

GAME CHEESEBURGER

We have hamburgers at home at least once a month, probably because of all the minced venison that we have on hand. Game mince is lean, but it has a great flavour. A little trick in this recipe adds moisture – as well as some vegies, which our kids might otherwise avoid. This trick also works for a sausage roll filling (see page 98) if you'd like to use game mince.

SERVES 5

For the patties, place a frying pan over a high heat and add the oil, onion, carrot and zucchini. Cook the vegies for 5–7 minutes, or until they reduce in bulk and have a slight colour. Fold the breadcrumbs through.

Place the mixture in a food processor and blend until it forms a paste. Transfer to a bowl, then set it aside to cool.

Once cooled, add the meat, garlic and egg. Mix together by hand until the mixture starts to bind. Weigh the mixture, measure out the salt and mix it in. Form the mixture into five balls and set aside.

Warm up a frying pan, griddle or chargrill pan to a high heat. Once hot, add the mince balls, without overcrowding the pan – you'll probably need to cook them in several batches. Press down on the balls to form a patty shape for the burgers. Cook for 3–5 minutes, until golden brown and a little caramelised underneath. Flip the patties and cook for a further 3–5 minutes, then remove and leave to rest for 3 minutes.

While the patties are resting, lay out the burger halves and assemble the other burger ingredients to your liking. Stack a patty inside each burger and serve hot.

PATTIES

1½ tablespoons olive oil

1 brown onion, sliced

1 carrot, grated

1 zucchini (courgette), grated

50 g (1¾ oz) dried sourdough or panko crumbs

600 g (1 lb 5 oz) minced (ground) game

1 garlic clove, crushed

1 free-range egg

6 g (¼ oz) pure sea salt (1% of the weight of the meat)

TO SERVE

5 burger rolls, split in half

10 slices of high-melt American burger cheese (the thickly sliced dark yellow-orange stuff)

3 Pickled cucumbers (page 209), sliced

1½ tablespoons Mustard (page 200)

1½ tablespoons Tomato sauce (page 205)

Kewpie mayonnaise, for drizzling

WALLABY BAKED IN HAY

Baking food in hay might seem like something a bit left of centre, but it's been around for a long time. In ancient Ireland, early settlers wrapped meats such as wild game in hay before placing it in a *fulacht fiadh* – a cooking pit used since the Bronze Age.

SERVES 8

3 garlic cloves, peeled

2 French shallots, peeled

5 anchovy fillets

2 rosemary sprigs, leaves stripped

juice of 1 lemon

30 ml (1 fl oz) olive oil

1 whole wallaby, shanks removed

2 kg (4 lb 6 oz) 'biscuit' of pesticide-free hay (see note)

Preheat the oven to 180°C (350°F).

Place the garlic, shallots, anchovies, rosemary leaves, lemon juice and olive oil in a food processor and blend to a paste.

Rub the paste over the wallaby and season with salt and pepper.

Find a roasting tin deep that will be enough to hold the whole wallaby, and line the base with the hay. Heat up the base of the tray over a high heat until the hay starts to smoke, then remove it from the heat.

Place the wallaby in the middle of the hay, then bring the sides of the hay up and around to enclose the wallaby. Wrap the top as tightly as you can with foil.

Place the tray into the oven and bake the wallaby for 30 minutes.

Remove from the oven and leave the wallaby for 15–20 minutes to rest before you open the foil. This should cook the wallaby to medium, but with this method you can cook the meat further and it won't dry out.

I find the flavour of this dish lends itself to brassica vegetables, like broccoli – either steamed, or raw in a salad.

‡ **NOTE**
If you don't have access to a farm, most pet shops will sell hay.

KANGAROO TARTARE WITH GAME CHIPS

Tartare is a classic dish made with beef – usually the eye fillet – but I do also like it with venison heart or kangaroo. Kangaroo backstraps have that perfect balance of texture and flavour to make this dish stand out. This recipe can be made with any game meat – but just remember that this is a raw meat dish that will slightly cure with the acid from the pickled veg and lemon juice, so you must be very careful about the quality of the meat you choose. Make sure the utmost hygiene has been used to harvest the meat, and that it has been stored correctly.

SERVES 4

200 g (7 oz) kangaroo backstraps, finely diced

1 French shallot, finely diced

2 Pickled cucumbers (page 209), finely diced

2 tablespoons baby capers, drained

1 garlic clove, crushed

2 tablespoons finely chopped chives

20 ml (¾ fl oz) olive oil

juice of ½ lemon

2 large king edward potatoes, or other good chipping potatoes

rice bran oil, for frying

4 egg yolks

Place the kangaroo in a bowl. Add the shallot, cucumber, capers, garlic, chives, olive oil and lemon juice and combine. Season with salt and pepper, then set aside.

To make the game chips you will need a traditional mandoline but, if you don't have access to one, you can just make regular chips.

Set the corrugated blade of the mandoline over a bowl, cut down on the top of a potato, then rotate the potato to make a crisscross pattern. Once you have cut both potatoes, top them with water and rinse off the starch.

Heat up about 10 cm (4 in) of oil for frying – a wok is good is here. Once the oil has reached 170°C (340°F), add some of the chips, making sure not to crowd the oil. Fry in batches, if needed, for about 5–7 minutes, until crisp and golden brown, then remove and drain on paper towel.

To serve, spread the tartare mixture into four portions and spoon them onto each plate, forming a mound. Using the back of the spoon, squash down a small hole in the centre and place an egg yolk in each. Arrange the game chips on the side and serve straight away.

ROO-STRONIE

A play on minestrone, this is another dish I've pinched from friends. I met Phil and Jenny Newton when they were supplying me and fellow chef Matthew Evans with squabs for our market stall. Phil and I struck up a good friendship, and I was lucky enough to be invited to his hunting property. By Tasmanian standards it had a lot of game – wallaby, rabbit, hare, fallow deer and goat – and it was also the place I took my son Felix on his first hunting trip. This roo-stronie was served by Phil and Jenny for lunch that day.

SERVES 12

1 kangaroo tail, or 2 wallaby tails

4 litres (135 fl oz/16 cups) Game stock (page 210)

oil, for cooking

1 brown onion, diced

1 leek, white part only, diced

1 carrot, diced

2 celery stalks, diced

3 garlic cloves, crushed

5 tomatoes, seeded and diced

1 bouquet garni, made with a small bundle of herbs, such as rosemary, thyme, bay leaves and sage

1 bunch of flat-leaf (Italian) parsley, chopped

1 bunch of basil, chopped

Place the kangaroo tail in a stockpot and cover with the stock. Bring the stock to the boil, then turn the heat down to a steady simmer and cook for 3–4 hours, skimming the stock if required, until the meat strips off the bone.

Strain the stock and set it aside. Pick all the meat off the bones and set it aside as well.

Take the same pot, place it over a high heat with a touch of oil and start to sauté the onion, leek, carrot, celery and garlic. Cook until the vegies start to brown a little, then stir in the tomatoes and cook for a further 5 minutes.

Add the reserved stock, tail meat and bouquet garni and bring to the boil. Once boiling, turn the heat down to a simmer and cook for 20 minutes.

Add the parsley and basil, then cook for a final 2 minutes. Check the seasoning, then serve with some good sourdough bread.

KANGAROO BRAIN FRITTERS (A.K.A. SLIPPERY BOB)

I adapted this recipe from *The English and Australian Cookery Book* for the *Gourmet Farmer Afloat* series on SBS television. The cookbook in question was an old one, from convict times, so the recipe was a bit dated and raw, to say the least. I gave it a slight tweak at the time – and now I have given it a good nudge. Brain fritters are a great way to eat brains without having to confront the fact that you are eating brains. Oh, and the original recipe was cooked in emu fat.

MAKES 12

100 g (3½ oz/⅔ cup)
    self-raising flour

1 free-range egg

100 ml (3½ fl oz) milk

6 kangaroo brains (or any other
    brains you can get your hands on)

2 tablespoons chopped chives

bacon fat or lard, for cooking

lemon wedges, for serving

Weigh the flour into a bowl. Make a well in the centre with a fork. Add the egg and milk, then start to fold and beat the liquid into the flour to form a batter.

Once the batter is smooth with no lumps, add the brains and beat them in with the fork. Add the chives and season with salt and pepper.

Place a heavy-based frying pan over a high heat. Once hot, turn the heat down to medium. Add the fat or lard, then spoon little piles of the batter mixture around the pan, making sure not to crowd it. Cook the fritters for 2–3 minutes on each side, until golden brown. Remove the fritters and drain on paper towel.

Serve hot, with wedges of lemon.

This is the way I tan my hides. I find this method easy to follow as it involves using only one chemical, and it gives a good result. There is also a natural method using tree bark, but I haven't had great success with this, as well as other chemical methods using tanning chrome, which I find leaves a blue tint on the hide. I take my time when skinning the animal, so I don't need to scrape much flesh off the hide.

I've also found that an electric pressure washer helps in cleaning the hide before you tan it. And once you're finished, you can also clean the flesh part of the hide with an electric sander, or the thicker hides using an electric angle grinder with a sanding disc.

You'll find aluminium sulphate in most hardware stores, in the pool supplies section.

TANNING

You will need

- salt, for drying the hide
- non-iodised salt (free of anti-caking agents)

Tanning solution
- 375 g (13 oz) aluminium sulphate
- 825 g (1 lb 13 oz) non-iodised sea salt
  (free of anti-caking agents)
- 20 litre (5.2 gallon) plastic bucket
- 11 litres (2.9 gallons) water
- staple gun (optional)

Method

If you find that, when you have skinned your animal, there is still a lot of flesh and fat on the skin, you will need to scrape it off. This is done by rubbing a 2 mm (⅛ in) layer of non-iodised salt on the hide and letting it dry out for 5 days, away from direct sunlight to avoid shrinkage. Once done, soak the hide in a bucket of cold water to make it soft again. Remove the hide from the water and start to scrape the flesh side of the pelt using a fleshing knife. Continue this until the skin is all clear of the thin layer of flesh, and looks a bit rough and dull. Be very careful not to scrape down too much, and to not cut through the skin.

Next, weigh the aluminium sulphate and salt, place them in the bucket and add the water, stirring as you go. Place the pelt in the bucket and, using a non-reactive (plastic or wood) rod, poke the pelt to make sure it is submerged and thoroughly covered.

Place a cover over the bucket and repeat the process of stirring the pelt each day for 7 days.

On the eighth day, flush the bucket with fresh water while stirring to rinse the pelt. Remove the pelt from the bucket, stretch it out and attach it reasonably tightly to a board or wall using a staple gun – with the fur facing into your board or wall, and the flesh side facing out to the elements. (If you don't have a staple gun, you can attach the pelt with small nails, or make small holes in it and tie it up with string.) What you are trying to do is stretch the pelt out so that when it dries and shrinks, it gets tight and keeps flat, without any creases.

Let the pelt dry over a period of a week. It's best to dry it slowly and out of direct sunlight.

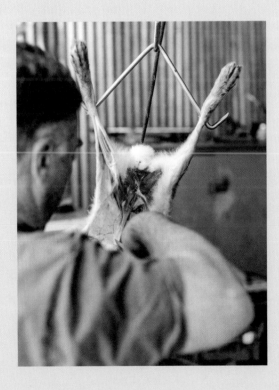

BUFFALO SCRUB BULL & BANTENG

Water buffalo are the premier game animal for international hunting in Australia, with overseas hunters heading to the northern parts of the continent to seek them out. Originating in India, South-East Asia and China, water buffalo today are also found in Europe, North America, South America and some African countries – with cape buffalo, which are a bigger species, also found in the eastern and southern parts of Africa.

In Australia, we also have scrub bulls, descended from domestic farm animals that ran loose and now breed in the wild. Then we have banteng, which were introduced from South-East Asia. Some are farmed, while others escaped and now range free in the wild.

They are all very similar to your typical beef cattle in terms of their muscle development, cuts and cooking methods, but free-ranging brings a different flavour.

BUFFALO / SCRUB BULL / BANTENG

LIST OF CUTS

1 Neck
twice-cooking
braising

2 Brisket
smoking low and
slow braising

Shoulder

3 Oyster blade (iron fillet)
grilling

4 Scotch
grilling
braising

5 Shanks
braising

6 Trim
mincing (grinding)

Middle

7 Backstrap/loin
grilling

8 Hanger (flank) steak
grilling

9 Skirt steak
grilling

10 Belly trim
mincing (grinding)

11 Eye fillets (tenderloin)
grilling
roasting

12 Ribs
twice-cooking
grilling
smoking low and slow

Haunch

13 Topside
roasting
grilling

14 Silverside
corning
roasting

15 Round
braising

16 Girello
curing

17 Rump cap
roasting
twice-cooking

18 Shanks
braising

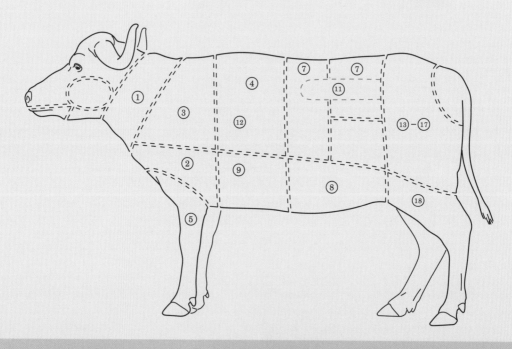

CHARCOAL-GRILLED BEEF WITH CHIMICHURRI

People have been cooking over fire since the dawn of time. There has been a massive trend towards it in city restaurants in recent years, but most hunters have never lost the skill. Once you add some chimichurri to your grilled meat, you'll never look back.

SERVES 4

1 hanger (flank) steak

1 red onion, sliced into 1–2 cm (½–¾ in) rings

150 g (5½ oz) green beans, topped and tailed

olive oil, for drizzling and cooking

100 g (3½ oz) wild rocket (arugula)

100 g (3½ oz) Chimichurri (page 207), plus extra to serve

Get your coals ready for cooking, with a grill plate on top. How to check the coals are ready for cooking, you might ask? It will depend on what type of wood you are using. What you are after is for the initial fire to die down and the wood to be burnt into coals. When you start to cook, the coals will flame up and start little fires, but to manage this is just a matter of moving the ingredients you are cooking to a cooler spot.

Place the steak, onion and green beans in a roasting tin, lightly drizzle with olive oil and season with sea salt flakes and freshly ground black pepper.

Once your coals are ready for cooking, start cooking the steak, onion and beans directly on the grill plate. Once the beans and onion have coloured,

remove them from the grill and place on your serving platter.

Then, once the steak is cooked to your liking, rest it on top of the onion and beans for 10 minutes, letting the juices flow onto the platter. I like my hanger steak pink or medium, so I cook it about 3–4 minutes on each side; I also turn it a few times, as I find this helps to char it up.

After the steak has rested, move it to a chopping board to slice for serving.

Toss the onion, beans and juices in a bowl with the rocket, then place back on the serving platter. Top with the sliced steak and dress with the chimichurri.

Serve hot, with a little extra chimichurri in a bowl for people to dollop on their plates if they desire.

BEEF BOURGUIGNON

I was once described as a chef who cooks like a French housewife. I took that as a huge compliment. This is a dish that I have prepared since the beginning of my time as a chef, but as I have evolved over the years, so has my execution of it. This is a great one for the camp cooker, to put on the morning coals, and come back to a hearty meal after a full day's hunting.

SERVES 4

oil and butter, for cooking

1 kg (2 lb 3 oz) oyster blade beef

12 button mushrooms, cut in half

6 French shallots, cut in half

1 carrot, diced

1 leek, white part only, diced

2 celery stalks, diced

3 bay leaves

3 thyme sprigs

200 g (7 oz) belly bacon (page 176), diced

1 bottle of red wine

Place a lidded heavy-based pan on the stove and bring to a high heat. Add some oil, season the pan with salt and pepper, then proceed to seal all the meat. Do this in batches, to make sure you get a golden colour all over the beef.

Set the meat aside, then colour the mushrooms and shallots. Once they are done, place them with the beef.

Add some butter and oil to the pan and cook the carrot, leek, celery, herbs and bacon for 7 minutes over a medium heat, until the vegetables soften.

Stir the meat, shallots and mushrooms back in. Add the wine and bring to the boil over a high heat, then reduce the heat to a rolling simmer.

Place the lid on and cook for 1 hour, or until the beef is tender, stirring occasionally to ensure the ingredients don't stick to the bottom of the pan.

Check the seasoning before you serve.

SHEPHERD'S PIE

A great family dinner, this one-pot wonder is a perfect way to introduce game meat to the family. Shepherd's pie is usually made with lamb, and cottage pie with beef, but you can use any minced game you like. And it's amazing the amount of veg you can hide in it for the kids.

SERVES 6

FILLING

olive oil, for cooking

700 g (1 lb 9 oz) minced (ground) game

1 brown onion, roughly chopped

2 garlic cloves

1 zucchini (courgette), roughly chopped

1 carrot, roughly chopped

2 celery stalks, roughly chopped

1 rosemary sprig

100 g (3½ oz/⅔ cup) peas, fresh or frozen

2 tablespoons tomato paste (concentrated purée)

1 tablespoon Worcestershire sauce (page 206)

150 ml (5 fl oz) Game stock (page 210) or chicken stock

TOPPING

700 g (1 lb 9 oz) good mashing potatoes, peeled and sliced

60 g (2 oz) butter

60 ml (2 fl oz) thickened (whipping) cream

To make the topping, place your potatoes in a pot with a good pinch of salt and cover with water. Bring to the boil, then reduce the heat to a simmer.

While the potatoes are cooking, start on the filling. Place some oil in a frying pan over a high heat and start to brown off the meat in batches. You want to colour the meat without stewing it, and make sure you season it as you go. Once the mince is browned, remove it from the pan and set aside in a bowl.

Add the onion, garlic, zucchini, carrot, celery and rosemary to the pan and cook over a medium heat until the vegies start to become soft; this should take around 10 minutes.

Remove from the heat, place the mixture in a food processor and blend into a paste.

Place the meat, and veg mixture back into the frying pan with the other ingredients and let them cook out for 15 minutes, stirring now and then. Check the seasoning and set aside.

Meanwhile, preheat the oven to 200°C (400°F).

When the potatoes are tender, drain them, then return them to the pan. Place them back on the stove and add the butter and cream. Using a potato masher, combine until smooth. Season and set aside.

Spoon the meat mixture into a deep baking dish. Top with the mashed potato and bake in the oven for 20 minutes, or until the top is golden brown.

Kids will see the peas, and can pick them out if needed – but all the other veg is puréed through the sauce and they are none the wiser.

This shepherd's pie goes great with a fresh salad.

RISSOLES WITH BACON & ONION GRAVY

Rissoles are standard Antipodean fare at any pub counter meal. I must admit I love a good rissole, but they have been mistreated over the years as an afterthought or a waste product from butchers' scraps. This recipe will hopefully restore your faith in an iconic dish.

SERVES 4

400 g (14 oz) minced (ground) beef

200 g (7 oz) minced (ground) pork

200 g (7 oz) minced (ground) goat

1 brown onion, roughly chopped

2 garlic cloves, roughly chopped

2 slices of sourdough bread

20 ml (¾ fl oz) olive oil

1 teaspoon salt

8 slices of belly bacon (page 176)

ONION GRAVY

50 g (1¾ oz) butter

3 brown onions, sliced

2 thyme sprigs

splash of red wine
(or vinegar if no wine is open)

2 tablespoons plain (all-purpose) flour

300 ml (10 fl oz) Game stock (page 210)

Preheat the oven to 140°C (285°F).

Place all the meats in a bowl and mix by hand to combine them.

Get a food processor and blend the onion, garlic, bread and olive oil to a paste.

Add the paste to the meat mixture and mix thoroughly by hand, or with a spatula. Season with the salt and some pepper, then form into eight balls.

Place a frying pan over a high heat and add the bacon. Cook until crispy on both sides. Remove the bacon, keeping the fat in the pan to cook the rissoles.

Place the meatballs into the pan, press down into a rissole shape and cook for 3 minutes on each side, until golden brown. Cook them in batches if your pan won't easily fit them all in one go.

Place the rissoles on a tray with the bacon on top, then place it in the oven to keep warm while you are making the gravy.

Add the butter and onion to the same pan and turn the heat down to medium. Slowly cook until the onion is translucent and starting to catch on the bottom of the pan; this should take around 15 minutes.

Stir in the thyme, then deglaze the pan with the red wine and cook for 1 minute. Add the flour and cook, stirring, for a further minute.

Add the stock and bring to the boil, then reduce the heat and simmer for 10–15 minutes, until the gravy coats the back of a spoon.

Serve the rissoles and bacon with the onion gravy poured over the top.

This dish is great with spuds of any type, or salad and chips (fries) pub-style.

OXTAIL SOUP

This soup – *sop buntut* – reminds me of Indonesia. I used to eat it regularly at one of our local warungs when I lived in Padang. Warungs are those little neighbourhood restaurants that you find scattered all over Indonesia, and a good one is like gold. We saw a lot of official-looking people frequenting one place, so we thought we'd give it a go. I loved this soup so much that I had to ask if they would show me how to cook it. As usual, they were more than happy and proud to show me some of their local recipes. A local friend came to help translate the recipe from the chef.

SERVES 4

4 French shallots, roughly chopped

4 garlic cloves, peeled

2 tablespoons fried shallots

1 tablespoon salt

1 tablespoon vegetable oil

400 g (14 oz) oxtail

5 small waxy potatoes (such as Dutch cream), cut into 2.5 cm (1 in) cubes

1 carrot, sliced

1 teaspoon ground white pepper

¼ teaspoon ground nutmeg

1 teaspoon beef stock powder

2 tablespoons chopped spring onion (scallion)

2 tablespoons chopped Asian celery leaves

Using a mortar and pestle, grind the French shallot, garlic, fried shallots and salt into a smooth paste, until evenly mixed.

Cook the paste, with the oil, in a frying pan over a medium heat until it becomes aromatic; this could be anywhere from 3–5 minutes. Set aside.

Place the oxtail in a lidded saucepan big enough to cover with 2 litres (68 fl oz/8 cups) of water. Bring to the boil over a high heat, then reduce to a slow simmer. Cook for 2–3 hours, checking that the level of the water doesn't drop too much, and skimming all the foam from the surface.

Once the meat is soft and is coming away from the bone, add the potato, carrot, fried spice paste, white pepper, nutmeg and stock powder, and half the spring onion and celery leaves. Cover and cook for 10–15 minutes.

Check the seasoning of the soup.

To serve, divide the oxtail among four bowls and top with the broth. Garnish with the remaining spring onion and celery leaves.

SMOKED BRISKET

4 kg (8 lb 13 oz) brisket, trimmed
  to your liking
100 g (3½ oz) Dry rub (page 209)

Whenever anyone talks about American-style barbecue, brisket is always at the top of the conversation. This recipe is a mix of what I can remember living there as a kid and what I have eaten over the years. For this, you will need a smoker, and these days there are so many different types and styles. I have an offset smoker now, but have had upright gas smokers in the past. Use the basic principles of this recipe and adjust them to your own equipment. Smoking the brisket is quite a long process, so make sure you have a good couple of days to do this.

MAKES 3 KG (6 LB 9 OZ)

Preheat the smoker to 100–110°C (210–230°F).

Place the brisket in a tub or bowl big enough for you to rub the dry rub all over it, then give the brisket a good rubbing all over with the mixture.

Place the brisket into the smoker. If your smoker is an offset one, make sure you place the thicker end of the brisket closer to the firebox.

Close the lid, then let it smoke until the internal temperature of the meat reads 50°C (122°F) on a meat thermometer; this should take about 3–4 hours.

Once the brisket has reached temperature, remove it and wrap in two layers of foil, making sure it is sealed at the sides. Place the brisket back into the smoker and continue to smoke it at the 100–110°C (210–230°F) mark for another 5–8 hours, until the internal temperature reaches 95°C (200°F).

Remove the meat and let it rest for at least 30 minutes before serving.

I love sliced brisket served with a side of pickles (page 209) and salad, to cut through the richness.

Any leftovers will keep for a few weeks in an airtight container in the fridge – and will last for a least a month if vacuum-packed. When you want to reheat the brisket, you can slice it and fry it like a steak, or wrap it in foil and place on a baking tray in a 120°C (250°F) oven for about 1 hour.

BEEF & STOUT PIES

A good pie with home-made pastry is hard to beat. Here, the filling is the classic combination of beef simmered in dark stout – but you can use this base recipe to mix and match the flavours using any game you like, from curried goat to kangaroo and venison.

MAKES 8 PIES

1 egg, beaten

PIE FILLING

butter and olive oil, for cooking

2.5 kg (5 lb 8 oz) beef topside, diced

3 brown onions, sliced

4 garlic cloves, sliced

2 thyme sprigs

2 rosemary sprigs

2 tablespoons plain (all-purpose) flour

440 ml (15 fl oz) stout

100 g (3½ oz/⅔ cup) peas, fresh or frozen

TOP PUFF PASTRY

250 g (9 oz/1⅔ cups) bakers flour

a good pinch of salt

250 g (9 oz) unsalted butter

100 ml (3½ fl oz) cold water

BOTTOM SHORTCRUST PASTRY

250 g (9 oz/1⅔ cups) bakers flour

a good pinch of salt

200 g (7 oz) butter, cubed and chilled

55 ml (1¾ fl oz) cold water

To make the filling, put a knob of butter and a slug of oil in a heavy-based saucepan and heat over a high heat. Brown the beef in batches, making sure not to crowd the pan, and seasoning the meat with salt and pepper. Once the meat is done, set it aside in a bowl that will catch all the juices.

Add some more butter and oil to the pan and turn the heat down low.

Add the onion, garlic and herbs and gently cook for 15–20 minutes, making sure they don't catch on the base of the pan. Stir in the flour and cook for a further 2 minutes. Add the beef and any juice from the bowl and stir them in.

Pour in the stout and bring to the boil, then turn the heat down to a slow simmer. Leave to cook for 45 minutes to 1 hour, stirring occasionally, until the beef is soft. Fold the peas through and check the seasoning. Leave to cool before using, or refrigerate overnight if making ahead.

To make the top puff pastry, sift the flour and salt into a large bowl. Rub in the butter using your fingers. Don't overdo it – you still want to see chunks of butter. Make a well in the centre, add the water and combine by hand to form a rough ball. All flours are different, so you might need a little more water to form the ball. Let the pastry rest for 5 minutes, then, on a lightly floured bench, roll it into a rectangle about 20 × 50 cm (8 × 19½ in). Fold the top third of the pastry into the centre, then fold the bottom third up over that. Place it back in the fridge and let it rest for another 5 minutes.

Repeat all the steps (rolling, folding, resting) another three times – that's four in total. Then let the pastry rest in the fridge for a final 20 minutes before using, or refrigerate overnight if making ahead.

To make the bottom shortcrust pastry, place the flour, salt and butter in a bowl. Using your fingers, rub the butter through the flour until you get a sand-like texture; this should take about 5 minutes. Pour in the cold water and bring together into a ball of dough. Put it on a lightly floured bench and knead for a minute. Place the dough back into the bowl, cover with a damp towel, and then into the fridge. Let the pastry rest for at least 1 hour before using, or overnight if making ahead.

When you're ready to bake, preheat the oven to 180°C (350°F), and grease eight pie tins. (I use traditional little metal pie tins that you can find in any kitchen supply store.)

To assemble the pies, roll out your bottom shortcrust pastry to 3 mm (⅛ in) thick, then cut out rounds to fit the pie bases. Make sure they are big enough to come up and hang over the sides; this will make it easier to seal the pies. Fill the pies with the meat mixture, up to the top of the pastry. Now roll out the puff pastry to 3 mm (⅛ in) and cut to fit the tops of the pies. Brush the pastry edges with the beaten egg to help them stick together, then press around the edges with your thumbs. Cut off the excess pastry and crimp the sides for presentation. Brush the tops with more egg wash.

Place the pie tins on a baking tray, then into the oven. (The tray will help keep the oven clean if any of the pies burst, or some filling leaks out. Trust me, cleaning burnt-on pie mix off the inside of an oven is not fun.)

Bake the pies for 20–25 minutes, or until the tops are golden brown. You might have to move the pies around to cook the pastry bases; make sure you lift the pies up with a cloth to check the pastry is cooked underneath.

Remove the pies from the oven and let them sit in the tins for 20 minutes before you try to take them out. I like to eat my pies with a smear of mustard (see page 200).

‡ **NOTE**
You can easily make the filling, top puff pastry and bottom shortcrust pastry the day before, and assemble the pies on the day of baking.

DRY-
AGEING
MEAT

It's a fact: if you hang meat, it becomes
tastier. Even leaving your harvest for
two weeks before eating produces a better
result. When you age meat, moisture
evaporates, leaving a bolder flavour, and
allowing the natural enzymes to break
down the connective tissue in the muscle,
making it more tender.

Hanging game meat is very different from hanging domestic farmed meat. Farmed animals are controlled with their feed and fencing – and sometimes what they are fed is not a natural part of their diet, such as corn being fed to livestock in America. And as farmed animals are kept between fences, or stuck in feedlots, their diets are controlled to yield a certain body weight within a certain time frame to make the animal viable for sale.

When I ran pigs for ten years as a primary producer, I took free-range to a different level, letting them move about in mobs as they would in the wild. They were fed on a daily basis, but also gained so much from what they dug up in the bush areas – and you could really see how what you put into the animal, and how physically active it is, changes its taste and texture. That's why the flavour of game meat is so varied, due to what the animal feeds on in its own local environment.

Also, most game meat is very light on fat, which means that when you are ageing it, you have to be very careful it doesn't dry out, as there is no fat to protect it – but there is also an upside to this, in that there is no fat to go rancid. Here in Australia, we are lucky that we can hunt a lot of the introduced species all year round, so we can pick the best time of year to harvest.

Ageing meat is a 'rabbit hole' of information. I'm going to list some of the key points, and I'll try to keep it as simple as possible.

This is for ageing your meat for tenderness, not dry-ageing.

I am not a massive fan of dry-ageing game for longer than 6 weeks, and I leave the pelt of the animal on most of the time – otherwise, you lose a lot of moisture from the meat, which causes loss of weight and shrinkage, and I find on game it can leave a bitter or liquorice taste on the meat.

I do hang game meat without the pelt to dry or set, but I don't leave it longer than 2 days.

Hygiene

When hanging meat, it cannot be stressed enough that you need to make sure you follow strict hygiene practices for all your preparation.

Make sure you use clean, sharp knives when field dressing, and clean them in between cuts. This is another reason why I wear disposable gloves during field dressing. Also, make sure you don't get fur in your cuts. And if you puncture the stomach, make sure you clean and wash the contents off before hanging the meat.

If you are hanging outside, or even in a cool room, you can – and most probably will – get mould spores pop up on the inside of your animal. You can wipe these off with a mild water and vinegar solution, which will discourage them from coming back.

133

Temperature

Once you get your carcass home, either in pieces or whole, you have to get the core temperature down.

You want to get the meat to 7°C (44.5°F) or lower, within 12–16 hours. This will stop the growth of mesophilic organisms. Mesophiles are micro-organisms that grow at moderate temperatures – 20–45°C (65–115°F) – with an optimum temperature range of 30–39°C (85–100°F). They are found in both soil and water environments. Then you have psychrophilic micro-organisms that are capable of growing and reproducing in low temperatures, ranging from –20°C to 10°C (5–50°F). Found in places that are permanently cold, psychrophiles (also called chryophiles) grow very slowly, and over time can make meat spoil.

I used to set my cool room at -2°C (28.5°F), and found I never had a problem with getting meat down to the right temperature, or getting mould. When I had it set at 2°C (35.5°F), after 2 weeks I would get *Penicillium candidum* (white mould) blooming in the chest cavity. This is a naturally occurring mould, and not a problem. You can remove it by wiping it down with a very watered-down vinegar and water solution.

In winter, I prefer to hang my animals outside whole, or in quarter pieces, because the temperature where I live drops below 0°C (32°F) at night, and sometimes won't climb past 10°C (50°F) during the day. I still prefer natural ageing outdoors rather than in cool rooms, but you need to keep a closer eye on the meat as the days rise in temperature – so if you can find a place in the shade with no sunlight, that will be ideal.

How to hang

I use stainless steel gambrels to hang all my carcasses, and stainless steel butchers' hooks for my pieces.

I hang all my whole carcasses from the back Achilles tendons and find it works well. I have tried tendon stretching, where you hang the carcass from the pelvis, and found not that much difference, although some people swear by it.

Make sure there is plenty of space around what you are hanging, and that it is not touching walls or other carcasses.

If you are hanging outside, a good game bag (made from a breathable fabric, e.g. cotton or muslin/cheesecloth) is needed.

134

How long

The length of time varies for each game animal.

You are not farming the animals and taking them at around the same age at the same time every year.

Sometimes you may get a big old stag or a maiden sow, or even a leveret (juvenile hare). This helps determine how long you need (or want) to hang the animal you have harvested. There is a zone beyond which I find further hanging is a waste of time, and that's at the 2–4 weeks mark. There is no reason to hang anything beyond 2 weeks if you are going to cut it up around the 4 week mark. All you are doing is losing weight on the animal.

If you are hanging past 4–6 weeks, well, you will get a development in taste, but not tenderness. All the tenderness and setting of the muscles will happen within 1–2 weeks.

That is why it is good to practise selective harvesting, to suit your meat preparation set-up.

If you don't have time for ageing, and you want to eat the meat you have harvested quickly, just freeze it overnight, then pull it out after it has frozen. Freezing kills the bacteria in the meat, and also breaks the protein molecules up, which makes the meat tender.

This simple list (see right) shows how long I hang my animals for, depending on the animal type, age and sex. I find the bigger males and the older females do have to hang longer, just because they have been working their muscles for a few more years than the younger animals. Having said that, I have eaten big stags weighing up to 350 kg (770 lb) two days after harvesting, and they have dressed out okay.

There are seasonal differences, too, due to what the animals are eating and the weather conditions at different times of the year – but you will have to understand your local environment to work out that info.

BIRDS
1–2 weeks

RABBIT
5 days

HARE
1–2 weeks

POSSUM
5 days

PIG

Slip – a piglet aged up to 6 weeks
2 days

Gilt – a maiden sow that hasn't reproduced
3–4 days

Sow – a sow aged over 12 months that has had young
5–7 days

Boar – a mature male
1 week

GOAT

Nanny
1 week

Buck
1–2 weeks

WALLABY

Doe
3–4 days

Buck
5 days

KANGAROO

Doe
5 days

Buck
1 week

CAMEL
1–2 weeks

BUFFALO
2 weeks

DEER

Fawn
3–5 days

Doe
1–2 weeks

Stag
2 weeks

N.06

DEER

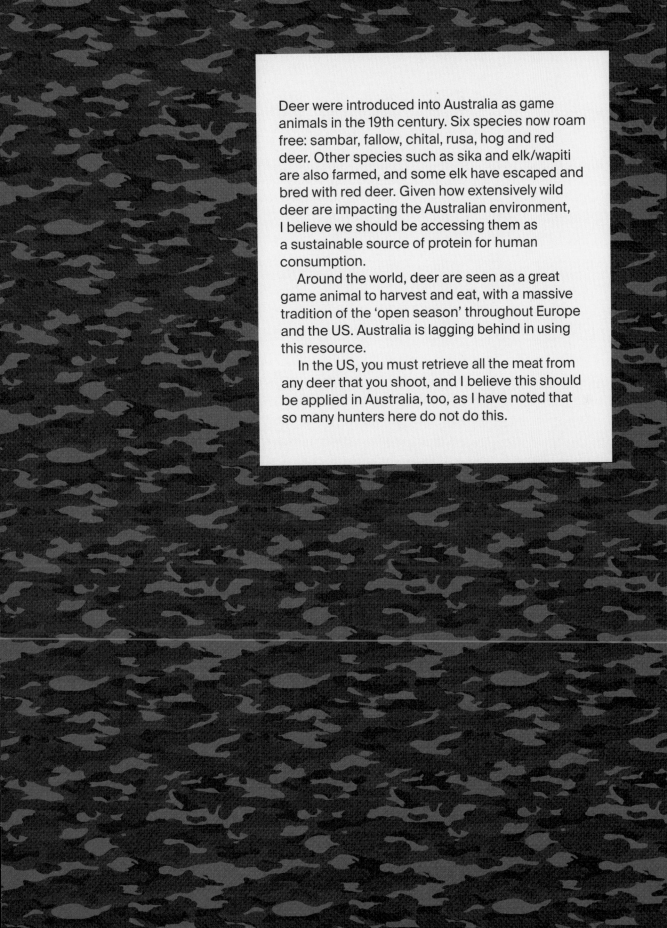

Deer were introduced into Australia as game animals in the 19th century. Six species now roam free: sambar, fallow, chital, rusa, hog and red deer. Other species such as sika and elk/wapiti are also farmed, and some elk have escaped and bred with red deer. Given how extensively wild deer are impacting the Australian environment, I believe we should be accessing them as a sustainable source of protein for human consumption.

Around the world, deer are seen as a great game animal to harvest and eat, with a massive tradition of the 'open season' throughout Europe and the US. Australia is lagging behind in using this resource.

In the US, you must retrieve all the meat from any deer that you shoot, and I believe this should be applied in Australia, too, as I have noted that so many hunters here do not do this.

DEER

LIST OF CUTS

1 **Neck**
twice-cooking
braising

2 **Brisket**
smoking low 'n' slow
mincing (grinding)
braising

Shoulder

3 **Oyster blade (iron fillet)**
grilling

4 **Scotch**
grilling
braising

5 **Shanks**
braising

Middle

6 **Backstrap/loin**
grilling

7 **Hanger steak**
grilling

8 **Skirt steak**
grilling

9 **Ribs**
grilling
twice-cooking

10 **Eye fillets (tenderloin)**
roasting
grilling

Haunch

11 **Topside**
grilling
roasting

12 **Silverside**
roasting
corning
braising

13 **Round**
dicing and braising

14 **Girello**
curing

15 **Rump cap**
twice-cooking, roasting

16 **Shank**
braising

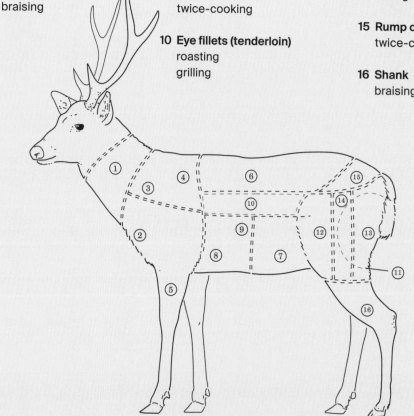

CAPING OUT A TROPHY MOUNT

If you want to have your animal turned into a trophy in memory of your hunt, you will need to prepare it in a certain way – a process known as 'caping out'.

There are a few different ways of caping out a deer for a shoulder mount, but it's best to speak to your taxidermist, who will tell you how they want to receive the deer pelt. This takes time to do in the field, so the meat will tend to sit there a lot longer before you harvest it. To keep the meat quality, bleed the animal by cutting the femoral artery in the back leg joint. This will give you the time you need to take care and make sure you don't rush it and damage the cape. This is a simple method that will give you both a cape that is ready for the taxidermist, and meat that is good for the table.

1   Use a boning knife to cut the femoral artery, by cutting into the inside of the back leg where it joins the pelvis. Once you cut the artery, let the leg hang open and bleed out.

2   Now cut a circle, skin depth only, all around the deer, just in front of the back legs.

3   Cut, skin depth only, straight up the backbone to the back of the head, level with the ears.

4   Cut both front hocks at the first join, and then 'sock' the legs. Do this by running your boning knife around the front leg to separate the skin from the pelt. You want to keep the front leg whole, without cuts, and this forms a little hood.

5   Start to skin the deer from the back, as normal.

6   Once you get it all skinned to the head, remove the head at the neck.

7   Take the head, with the 'cape' attached, to the taxidermist as soon as possible for them to complete the face caping.

Face caping

Face caping is the final stage of preparing your trophy for the tanning stage. This takes time, a very sharp scalpel and a great knowledge of the animal's facial anatomy. Most taxidermists will (and can) do this for you for an extra charge. If you aren't confident, get them to do it, as they would prefer not to cover up someone else's mistakes.

1   Using a sharp scalpel, cut to the bone at the top and bottom teeth, along the gums.

2   Then start to cut up around the gums, working up onto the nose.

3   Do the bottom side and work around the bottom jaw.

4   Be careful up around the scent ducts (if the animal has some; they'll be just below the eyes). Continue working until just before the eyes.

5   Cut over the eyes, and stop at the top of the skull.

6   Cut at the back of the head in a 'Y' fashion, towards the horns.

7   Cut around the base of the pedicle (at the bottom of the antlers) where it meets the fur. Now cut up the incision you did towards the horn.

8   Tap a screwdriver up around the pedicle to remove the hair from around the base.

9   Cut up the side of the horn to remove the hair from the antler bases.

10 Salt the cape with a 2–3 mm (⅛–⅙ in) layer of pure salt (non-iodised, and free of anti-caking agents), and roll with the skin side outwards. Take straight away to a taxidermist.

GRILLED VENISON HEART

True story: I once conducted a taste test of venison heart versus venison eye fillet, preparing each of them raw, as a tartare. It was a blind tasting, so no one knew what cuts I used. The venison heart came out on top, to everyone's surprise.

SERVES 6

1 venison heart
olive oil, for grilling
Green sauce (salsa verde) (page 206)

Trim the heart up for grilling (see photo on page 40).

Warm a frying pan or griddle pan over a high heat, or you can cook this on a barbecue.

Put the heart on a plate, lightly cover with oil, then season with salt and pepper.

Place the heart in the pan or on the grill and cook on one side for 2–3 minutes, then turn and repeat on the other side. Remove from the grill and set aside to rest for 3–5 minutes.

While the heart is resting, check the seasoning of the green sauce.

To serve, slice the heart into nice thin strips and arrange on a plate, then drizzle the green sauce over.

This is a great tapas or share-plate dish, as most people will only want to try a little bit of it.

144

TWICE-COOKED VENISON SCOTCH WITH ANCHOVY, LEMON, THYME & GARLIC

1 venison scotch fillet
3 garlic cloves, crushed
3 anchovy fillets, chopped
8 thyme sprigs
juice of 1 lemon
90 ml (3 fl oz) olive oil

If you can't cook something right, then cook it twice, I say. I use this technique all the time, for all types and cuts of game. I love the texture and the flavour twice-cooking gives. Rump cap is another one of my favourite cuts for this dish. We regularly have it as a family, cooked over coals, then placed in the middle of the table for everyone to make their own tacos or flatbread kebabs. This is also a great main for a dinner, with any side dishes you like.

SERVES 5

Place the venison in a food vacuum-sealer bag or zip-lock bag and place it in a lidded pot deep enough to cover it with water. (If you have a *sous vide* machine, use that instead.) Bring the water to the boil, then turn the heat down to the lowest simmer possible and place the lid on.

Cook the venison for 3–4 hours, until you can feel the meat protein starting to break apart. (You can do this by touch – just make sure you don't burn your hands.)

Turn the heat off, remove the lid and let the venison stand in the bag for 1 hour.

Remove the venison from the bag and place it in a bowl. There will be a lot of stock (meat juice) left in the bag, which can be used in any soups or braises, as it's full of flavour (you can freeze it).

Now add all the other ingredients to the bowl and toss the venison around in the marinade. Let it sit in the marinade for at least 30 minutes.

Fire up your charcoal barbecue and get it ready for cooking. Place the venison onto the grill and cook for about 20 minutes, turning to make sure you crisp and colour the outside. While the venison is cooking, make sure you season all sides of the meat with salt and pepper.

Once it's ready, place the whole piece on the table, carve off chunks and enjoy.

PULLED VENISON NECK

If I take food on a hunt, there's a good chance I'm taking this dish. The neck is a major working muscle, so it has superb flavour. It does take a long time to cook, but once it does, it just pulls apart. It's so versatile you can eat it in a roll or with rice – and better yet, cold, like rillettes on a charcuterie board.

SERVES 8

800 g (1 lb 12 oz) boned-out venison neck meat

2 tablespoons plain (all-purpose) flour

3 tablespoons dripping or lard

1 brown onion, sliced

5 garlic cloves, crushed

200 ml (7 fl oz) red wine

400 ml (13 ½ fl oz) Game stock (page 210) or chicken stock

5 juniper berries

3 fresh bay leaves

2 thyme sprigs

Take a heavy-based saucepan with a fitted lid and place it over a high heat.

On a plate, dust the venison neck in the flour and season with salt and pepper.

Add the dripping to the pot, then follow with the venison. Colour each side of the venison and remove it from the pot.

Cook the onion and garlic in the dripping for 5 minutes, or until the onion starts to become translucent. Add the wine, then the stock, juniper berries and herbs.

Lastly, place the venison on top and bring the stock to the boil. Turn the heat down to a steady simmer and place the lid on. (If you don't want to cook it on the stove, you can also put the pot in a preheated 160°C/320°F oven, but make sure your pot is ovenproof.)

After 4 hours, check the meat by pressing it with tongs. If it starts to pull apart, you are done; if not, cook it until it does.

Remove the meat and start to pull it apart in a bowl. Strain the sauce, then slowly add a little bit back to the meat to keep it moist.

I've served this dish around a campfire with smashed pink-eye potatoes, cabbage and mushrooms – a great finish to a long day's hunting.

VENISON & BLACK BEAN EMPANADAS

Whenever I make empanadas, there are never enough. I used to make them the South American way, with pastry, and bake them like little pasties. But after trying them with fresh home-made corn tortillas, I haven't looked back. Yes, they are gluten free – but unlike many gluten-free recipes, these taste great. You will need a tortilla press, which you can find quite easily, and can use for making dumplings and poppadoms, too. You'll need to soak the black beans overnight, so start a day ahead.

MAKES 18–20

100 g (3½ oz) dried black beans, soaked overnight

400 g (14 oz) venison, finely diced or coarsely minced (ground)

3 French shallots, sliced

3 garlic cloves

2 tomatoes, seeded and chopped

2 tablespoons sweet paprika

1 tablespoon ground cumin

1 tablespoon ground coriander

2 spring onions (scallions), chopped

200 ml (7 fl oz) frying oil, such as rice bran

TORTILLA DOUGH

450 g (1 lb) masa flour

350 ml (12 fl oz) warm water

148

Place the beans in a pot, cover with cold water, add a pinch of salt and bring to the boil. Once boiling, turn the heat down to a rolling simmer and cook for 15 minutes, or until the beans are soft. Remove from the heat and strain the beans – but reserve the liquid.

Brown off the meat in a large frying pan in some oil; do this in batches if there is not enough space, and make sure you season the meat with salt and pepper. Set the meat aside.

In the same pan, cook the shallot and garlic over a medium heat until they become translucent. Add the tomatoes and spices and cook for a further minute.

Add the meat and beans, then top up the pan with a bit of the reserved bean cooking liquor – you want to keep this mixture moist but not wet. Now cook for 5–10 minutes, or until reasonably thick. Stir in the spring onion and remove from the heat. At this stage, check the seasoning, then set it aside to cool.

To make the tortilla dough, weigh out your masa flour into the mixing bowl of an electric stand mixer (or you can mix by hand if you want). Add a pinch of salt and turn the mixer on to low. Add 250 ml (8½ fl oz/1 cup) of the warm water and start to bring the mix together, then slowly add the remaining 100 ml (3½ fl oz) water until you get the right consistency. Check this by rolling a little bit of dough, then pressing it between your thumb and forefinger: if it squishes out without cracking on the edges, it's good.

Remove the mixture and knead by hand for 20 seconds. Place the dough ball back into the mixing bowl, cover with a damp towel and leave to rest for 30 minutes.

To assemble the empanadas, cut the dough into quarters. I find with boiled water pastry there is no need to flour the bench – but if you like, you can lightly dust your bench to start. Roll each quarter into a long cylinder about 2.5 cm (1 in) thick, then cut each into five portions. Roll each piece into a little ball, place them back in the bowl and cover with a damp towel. (With this pastry, you want to work with one piece at a time, because when it dries out it cracks badly.)

Cut two pieces of baking paper to use on each side of your tortilla press, then take a little ball of dough and place it in the middle. Press down to make a tortilla. Remove the top piece of paper and, grabbing the bottom piece, peel this off into the palm of your hand. Place a tablespoon of the meat mixture in the middle of the tortilla while it's still in your palm, then close over the tortilla to create a half-moon shape. Gently crimp around the edge to seal it, then place on a flat tray and cover with a moist towel. Repeat this process until all the empanadas are done.

To cook them, take a large heavy-based frying pan deep enough to hold 1 cm (½ in) of oil and place it over a high heat until the temperature reaches 180°C (350°F). Once hot, place a batch of empanadas in, making sure not to overlap them. Fry on each side for 3–4 minutes, or until golden in colour, then remove and drain on paper towel. Continue until they are all cooked.

Serve the empanadas warm, with home-made hot sauce or salsa.

VENISON TONGUE TACOS

Tacos are the ultimate street food. To me, authentic street food is not about using mainstream cuts of meat. In my travels, I have found that street vendors will often use the lesser known cuts, I guess because they're more economical and readily available. I had a beef tongue taco one time and it absolutely blew my mind – the flavour and texture were on point. Here I've replaced the beef tongue with a venison tongue and it's a ripper.

SERVES 6

1 sambar deer tongue (or 3 fallow deer tongues)

400 ml (13½ fl oz) Game stock (page 210)

¼ white cabbage, shredded

1 red chilli, seeded and sliced

1–2 red onions, thinly sliced

2 avocados, sliced

1 bunch of coriander (cilantro), picked

lemon or lime, for squeezing

Fermented chilli sauce (page 204)

TORTILLA DOUGH

450 g (1 lb) masa flour

a pinch of salt

350 ml (12 fl oz) warm water

Place the tongue in a pot deep enough to cover it with stock. Pour in the stock. Bring to the boil, then reduce the heat to a rolling simmer. (At this stage, if you want, you can add some onion, garlic and bay leaf – but I prefer just to cook the tongue in a good stock.)

Cover the tongue with a cartouche (a paper lid; see page 14).

Cook the stew at a rolling simmer for 3–4 hours, topping up the stock if needed, until the skin peels off the tongue when tested with a pair of tongs. Remove from the heat and let the tongue cool down before you peel it.

To make the tortilla dough, weigh out your masa flour into the mixing bowl of an electric stand mixer (or you can mix by hand if you want). Add a pinch of salt and turn the mixer on to low. Add 250 ml (8½ fl oz/1 cup) of the warm water and start to bring the mix together, then slowly add the remaining 100 ml (3½ fl oz) water until you get the right consistency. Check this by rolling a little bit of dough, then pressing it between your thumb and forefinger: if it squishes out without cracking on the edges, it's good.

Remove the mixture and work by hand for 20 seconds. Place the dough ball back into the mixing bowl, cover with a damp towel and leave to rest for 30 minutes.

Once rested, cut the dough into quarters. I find this doesn't need a floured bench, but go ahead if

you like. Roll each quarter into a long cylinder about 2.5 cm (1 in) thick, then cut each into five portions. Roll each piece into a little ball, place them back in the bowl and cover with a damp towel. (With this pastry, you want to work with one piece at a time, because when it dries out it cracks badly.)

Cut two pieces of baking paper to use on each side of your tortilla press, then take a little ball of dough and place it in the middle. Press down to make a tortilla.

Preheat a frying pan to a low heat. Remove the top piece of paper and, grabbing the bottom piece, lay the tortilla, naked side down, in the frying pan. Peel the back of the paper and cook the tortilla for 2 minutes, or until it puffs up, then turn it over and cook the other side.

Remove the tortilla and wrap it in a towel on a plate to keep it warm and out of direct air, as this will make it go stale.

Repeat until all the tortillas are cooked.

To assemble the tacos, take your cooled tongue and slice it as thinly as possible. Place a few slices in the middle of your tortilla, then top with a little cabbage, chilli, onion, avocado and coriander, and add a quick dash of citrus juice and hot sauce.

Eat immediately. Then eat another.

VENISON BBQ RIBS

A lot of hunters leave the ribs on the carcass in the bush, but I don't understand why. My kids love a good feed of venison ribs, probably because they can use their hands to eat them. Like most recipes, this is a simple template for you to take further; it's the technique here that will help. You can cook the ribs on a barbecue, over charcoal or under an oven grill (broiler) – whichever method you choose, they will turn out great.

SERVES 4

1 full venison rib cage, spilt into 4
50 g (1¾ oz) Dry rub (page 209)
200 ml (7 fl oz) BBQ sauce
    (page 205)

Preheat the oven to 150°C (300°F).
    Take the ribs and place them in a roasting tin. Cover the ribs with the dry rub mixture and add 100 ml (3½ fl oz) of the barbecue sauce. Cover the tray with foil, making sure it seals tight, with no holes.
    Bake the ribs for 1½–2 hours. Remove from the oven and leave to cool.
    Once cooled, remove the ribs from the tray, then heat up the sauce you cooked the ribs in.
    Once your sauce is hot, start cooking the ribs. While there is one side down cooking, get a basting brush and brush the remaining barbecue sauce on the upper side of the ribs.
    Cook the ribs for 5 minutes on each side, turning and basting as you go, until they are golden and a bit sticky.
    Serve the ribs straight off the grill, with a good slaw, and maybe corn if it's in season.

WHOLE GRILLED VENISON TOPSIDE WITH SPAETZLE, SILVERBEET & MUSTARD GRAVY

Here's a complete dish for a winter's evening. Spaetzle is a great accompaniment for any game, but I love it with venison. A German dumpling that's tossed in butter with silverbeet will satisfy anyone in cold weather.

SERVES 6

1 venison topside

oil, for cooking

100 g (3½ oz) butter

2 tablespoons plain (all-purpose) flour

100 ml (3½ fl oz) Game stock (page 210)

2 tablespoons Mustard (page 200)

1 tablespoon chopped chives

3 French shallots, sliced

2 garlic cloves, crushed

1 bunch of silverbeet (Swiss chard), washed and shredded

SPAETZLE

375 g (13 oz) plain (all-purpose) flour

a pinch of salt

a pinch of ground white pepper

1 teaspoon ground nutmeg

6 free-range eggs

195 ml (6½ fl oz) milk

Preheat the oven to 170°C (340°F).

To make the spaetzle, mix together the flour, salt, pepper and nutmeg in a bowl. In a separate bowl, beat the eggs well, then add the milk and stir into the flour mixture until a smooth paste forms. Set aside.

Bring 1 litre (34 fl oz/4 cups) water to the boil with a good pinch of salt. Once boiling, press the spaetzle dough through a large-holed sieve or potato ricer, into the water. Once the dumplings float, which should take around 2 minutes, remove them with a slotted spoon and cool the dumplings down in an ice bath.

I like to fully cook my venison topside on a charcoal barbecue, but this does take a long time and it's not that easy until you know how to do it. For this recipe, season and oil the venison in a roasting tin and place the roasting tin under your hot grill (broiler). Grill on each side for 5 minutes, or until you get good colour, and don't be shy with the salt and pepper.

Place the roasting tin in the oven and cook the venison for 15 minutes, then remove from the oven, wrap the venison in foil and leave to rest for 7 minutes. This should be enough to cook the venison on the medium–rare to medium side.

Put the venison on your carving board. Place the roasting tin back over a medium heat with half the butter in. Once the butter has melted, stir in the flour and let it cook out for 1 minute, then stir in the stock and bring to the boil. Once boiling, stir in the mustard. Check the seasoning, fold the chives through and remove the gravy from the heat.

Get a heavy-based frying pan over a high heat. Add the remaining butter and sauté the shallot and garlic for 1 minute. Toss in the spaetzle and continue to sauté until the spaetzle takes on a golden brown colour.

Toss the silverbeet in and cook for a couple of minutes, keeping it moving in the pan. Once the silverbeet has broken down, check the seasoning and spoon onto a serving platter.

Slice the venison and arrange on the serving platter. Drizzle with the mustard gravy, reserving any remaining gravy on the side.

ROASTED SADDLE OF VENISON ON THE BONE, WITH BONE MARROW SAUCE

1 saddle of venison

olive oil, for drizzling

5 French shallots, sliced

2 garlic cloves, crushed

2 thyme sprigs

3 juniper berries, cracked

100 ml (3½ fl oz) red wine

300 ml (10 fl oz) Game stock (page 210) or chicken stock

50 g (1¾ oz) bone marrow

This one came about from a hare dish I used to do in London. When you cook meat on the bone, as you do here, it's a different beast. It takes a bit more skill – but the flavour is sweeter, and when rested right, the meat is so tender. When you cook this dish, bring it to the table and carve it in front of your friends. It's quite the spectacle for a dinner party.

SERVES 8

Preheat the oven to 200°C (400°F).

Grab a frying pan large enough to fit the venison saddle and place it over a high heat (see note).

Give the venison a solid seasoning with sea salt and freshly ground black pepper and rub with olive oil. Place it in the pan, presentation side down (bones facing up). Seal both sides of the saddle on the top to a golden brown, which should take about 3–4 minutes each side.

Place the venison saddle in a roasting tin, with the bones facing down, presentation side up. Roast for 15 minutes, then turn it over and cook for a further 5 minutes.

Remove from the oven. Leaving it uncovered, let the venison rest in the tray, with the loins still facing down, for 10 minutes. Then put the saddle on your chopping board, ready to slice in another 20 minutes.

Meanwhile, place the roasting tin back over a high heat. Add the shallot, garlic, thyme and juniper berries and cook for 2 minutes. Deglaze the pan with the red wine and let it reduce for 1 minute.

Stir in the stock and cook the sauce down for 5–10 minutes, or until it starts to thicken a little.

Add the bone marrow and stir it in, to help thicken the sauce and also give a rich texture (this is called monter au beurre, which translates as 'mounting with butter'). Once the bone marrow is emulsified, which should only take about 1 minute, set the sauce aside, but keep it warm.

Slice the meat off the saddle and arrange it on a platter. Dress with the bone marrow sauce and serve with green beans and roast potatoes.

‡ **NOTE**
If you don't have a frying pan big enough to hold the venison saddle, just brown it on your barbecue plate.

THE RUT

This is the part of the hunting season that gets a lot of hunters twitching – when the stags get all silly and mate for several weeks. During this time, most stags are off their guard, too busy thinking about all the does and punching on with any other male that steps into their zone. The rut also affects goats.

Hunters find this time great as they can get really close, and also see what's around the area trophy-wise. At this time, the stags fight and urinate all over themselves to spray their scent around. Their testosterone is off the charts, they don't feed, and they lose a lot of condition, so with most of the stags that are hunted at this time, only their heads are taken, and the meat is left behind. Besides the fact that the stags aren't in condition, they have a strong smell and slight taint to the meat, due to their abnormal hormonal balance.

At this time, it's a case-by-case approach. One year I harvested a fallow stag that was mid rut; he was malformed with one testicle, so he wasn't that stinky, and had big swollen neck muscles from all his bellowing and croaking, trying to attract the ladies. I used him as I would any other deer, and his meat was fine.

The average rutting stag's meat is fine once you get past the aroma of the animal, but sometimes there is a strong taste in the meat. I found that when I was field dressing the stag, trimming the meat away from the carcass, all the glands were swollen and spread out through the meat much more than normal. When butchering, taking extra care to remove the glands will help with the flavour of the meat being less gamey.

Another trick I have used with rutting red deer is to soak the meat in red wine with some herbs and spices for a week; I use juniper berries, garlic, rosemary, thyme, black peppercorns and shallots. This extracts all the funkiness from the meat, and leaves you with a clean-tasting piece of venison. This method also works with meat that hasn't bled well from a misplaced shot.

On a hunt with Felix

SAUSAGES & CHARCUTERIE

I used to be a pig farmer and made smallgoods
from the pigs as my sole income for ten years.
My nickname was Rossage as I used to make
dozens of kilos of fresh sausages a week and
sell out most, if not every, week. It's amazing
the versatility of a humble sausage, be it for
breakfast, lunch or dinner. And when you use
cuts and not trim, it takes them to the next level.
Everywhere in the world has its own variety of
sausage that has been a part of the regional
cuisine that everyone has grown up with.
Charcuterie goes hand in hand with any type of
meat preparation. Many people think there is a
mystical process that helps your meat ferment
and cure for consumption, but it's really not that
hard. These recipes will give you confidence
in attempting and mastering this process so
you can impress people with your skills. It will
also help make the most of your hunting spoils,
preserving the harvest for years to come.

SAUSAGE & CHARCUTERIE BASICS

Homemade sausages

Making your own sausages and charcuterie is actually not as hard as it looks and sounds, but you will need the right tools for the job – and good hygiene is a big must. There are a few rules you need to follow, but the guidelines on the next few pages will help you achieve good results, without going through the heartbreak of failure.

Sausage-making equipment

Mincer (grinder)

I have a self-standing meat mincer (grinder) that sits on the benchtop and is not attached to an electric mixer. Generally, I use an #8 (8 mm/⅓ in) or #10 (10 mm/½ in) blade for mincing (grinding) meat.

Sausage cannon

I would recommend using a sausage cannon that's at least 5 kg (11 lb) in size. I prefer the vertical models, as these are easier to hold down while you are pumping out the sausages.

Natural sausage casings

I like to use natural sausage skins, as I find they cook and taste better than collagen or synthetic ones. When air-drying sausages, they also breathe better, curing the meat evenly. You can buy these sausage casings online at many retailers, or from your local butcher supplies store. They come in sizes numbered with the range of their diameter. So, 32–35 means the casings are 32–35 mm (1¼–1½ in) in diameter, for example. The larger part of the intestines is called a 'bung'; these will be larger than other sausage casings, and are used for making mortadella and big salamis. These are also available from online retailers and butcher supplies shops.

Starter culture

You can buy this from most butcher or sausage supplies shops, and online. Starter cultures (such as Bactoferm) are a freeze-dried form of beneficial bacteria that are added to sausage mixes to help the natural fermenting and curing process and minimise any risk of spoilage by harmful bacteria. Using a starter culture gives you peace of mind that the right bacteria are inoculated into your sausages before you hang them to dry.

Cure salt #1

Also known as pink salt and Prague powder, curing salt helps prevent the growth of dangerous bacteria when making salami. Some people believe it also gives a better flavour to the finished product. You can buy it online from sausage supplies shops.

Meat netting

This can be used for netting hams and charcuterie. It is also handy for cooking things like shoulder roasts. You'll find it in sausage supplies shops.

Salami pricker

You can buy these, or make one with wood and some clean nails hammered through. Using this on your salamis before they cure will help the meat breathe, to help the natural fermentation along.

Plastic tubs for mixing meat

Kitchen cutting boards

Hygiene is everything

- Wash your hands regularly during the process of making these products, or wear a pair of disposable food-safe gloves.
- Sterilise all your equipment before you start. Baby bottle sanitisers work well for this.
- Before starting, freeze all your meat mincer parts, after sanitising them first, for at least 20 minutes. It's best to work as cold as possible, as this helps with mincing. When the mincing machine and blades get hot, it will tear the meat.
- Use non-reactive tubs and bowls (plastic, glass and stainless steel), so they don't rust or oxidise.

2

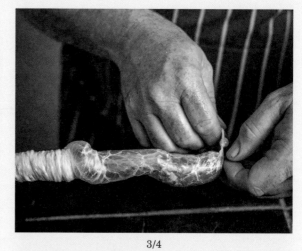

3/4

4

5

Sausage pumping & filling

1 Before making sausages, ensure your sausage
   cannon is washed and sanitised.

2 Pre-soak your sausage casings in tepid
   (room temperature) water for at least 20 minutes
   before you start to use them. This will make the
   casings easier to slide onto the nozzle of your
   sausage cannon.

3 Once soaked, slide the sausage casing onto your
   nozzle, then attach the nozzle to your sausage
   pump. Add the filling into the top of the cannon,
   making sure you pack it down to avoid air bubbles,
   as you don't want these in your sausages.

4 Start to pump the filling out through the nozzle.
   Once it starts to come out, stop, pull the casing
   over the end and tie a double knot in it, then start
   to fill the sausage. You want the sausages to be
   filled just right – this will take a bit of practice.
   If you under-fill the sausages, they will be baggy
   and won't have the right size or structure, and if
   you over-fill them, they will burst when you twist
   them to make the links. I find it helpful having my
   thumb and forefinger on the end of the nozzle to
   help the sausage feed out.

5 Start to fill the sausage out onto your bench – and
   when the mixture is pumped through, don't tie the
   end until you finish your twisting.

166

5

6

7

7

6   I am going to try to explain the sequence of twisting, which is kind of like patting your head and rubbing your tummy at the same time. First, make a loop from the end that is tied.

7   Twist the loop clockwise three times, then pass the rest of the sausage up through the loop.

8   Once it has reached the same size as the loop, pinch it at the top, and pass the sausage up and through the junction of the three sausages. When the sausage passes up, start the loop again and repeat what you just did.

9   Once the sausages are tied, tie a knot in the end sausage.

10 Hang the sausages for at least 3–4 hours – preferably overnight. This lets the sausages rest and set, so they won't split when you start to fry them.

A place to hang: air drying

Finding a good hanging place for your charcuterie is key. I used to hang mine from the roof in an old apple shed – after I'd put in a false roof, as I found animals were coming from the rafters, dropping down the line and eating the top of my hams and salamis!

You can convert any shed or fridge into a hanging space, but make sure there are some walls made of mesh or fly wire, as you need a good draught of air to come through and circulate around the charcuterie. If you can afford a special curing fridge or wine fridge, even better.

If you want to try the traditional way of hanging outdoors, here are a few tips:

- Hanging is best at 12°C (53.5°F), with some humidity. Hanging damp towels or placing bowls of water around will help create a bit of humidity.
- Depending on your local climate, mid-autumn to mid-spring are generally best, being cooler and wetter. In Australia, May to October are the wetter, cooler months.
- You need a spot that has good air circulation – but not subjected to a strong breeze, as this will dry your charcuterie out.
- Make sure your charcuterie is rodent, insect and wasp proof. You can do this by wrapping it in muslin (cheesecloth), or making sure the space has great mesh to let the air in but keep the nasties out.

Ham and bacon

CONFIT QUAIL

Confit is a technique of cooking that lends itself to birds on the bone. The main difference between confit and rillettes (page 174) is that confit leaves the pieces whole and with the bone in, whereas rillettes feature meat that is shredded off the bone. Nowadays people confit many different types of protein, and even vegetables – but in France, where the method originates, duck legs are still the main confit dish. Whole quails are just the right size, and twice-cooking them makes them melt in the mouth.

SERVES 6

6 whole quails
100 g (3½ oz) sea salt flakes
1 litre (34 fl oz/4 cups) duck fat
1 brown onion, quartered
5 sage leaves
5 juniper berries, crushed
3 garlic cloves, crushed
1 tablespoon black peppercorns

Place the quails in a plastic container, generously rub them with the salt, then cover and refrigerate for 12 hours.

Remove the quails from the fridge, rinse off the salt, then pat dry with paper towel. Place the quails in a large saucepan deep enough to cover them when you pour in the duck fat.

Add the duck fat, onion, sage, juniper, garlic and pepper and bring to the boil, then reduce the temperature to a rolling simmer and cook for 4 hours. To check the quails, just pinch a whole bird between your fingers, and it should have some 'give' in the meat. Be careful not to overcook the quails – you don't want them falling apart.

Remove the quails from the cooking liquor and place them in a roasting tin to cool down. Strain the cooking liquid, then place it in your fridge or freezer to use again. (I find bird fat is great in pastry, and also makes for incredible roast potatoes. Slow-braising some brussels sprouts with garlic in the fat is another winner.)

Meanwhile, preheat the oven to 200°C (400°F).

Place the quails into the hot oven and roast for 10 minutes, or until crispy and brown. Serve hot, with a fresh green salad.

‡ NOTE
You'll need to start this dish the day before.

RABBIT TERRINE

A terrine is a meat farce, which is a fancy term for minced meat bound together – or you could also call it a dressed-up meatloaf. Terrines are great to take as a lunch in the field, as they pack light and are very filling. For this recipe you will need a meat mincer; there are many options out there for the home cook. I prefer to use a hand-crank mincer for my rabbit terrines.

MAKES ABOUT 1 KG (2 LB 3 OZ)

2 whole wild rabbits,
   or 1 whole farmed rabbit
   (about 1.5–2 kg/3 lb 5 oz–4 lb 6 oz)

20 g (¾ oz) butter

20 ml (¾ fl oz) olive oil

3 French shallots, sliced

2 garlic cloves, crushed

1 thyme sprig

1 rosemary sprig

1 bay leaf

200 g (7 oz) pork shoulder, diced

1 tablespoon chopped flat-leaf
   (Italian) parsley

½ teaspoon ground
   white pepper

sea salt flakes (1% of the overall
   weight of the terrine mixture)

TO LINE THE MOULD

100 g (3½ oz) caul fat, backfat
   or thinly sliced streaky bacon

Take the rabbit, remove the backstraps and kidneys, trim and slice them into long strips, then place them on a tray in the fridge. Next, bone out the rest of the meat from the rabbit for mincing (grinding), place in a stainless steel bowl and refrigerate.

Heat the butter and oil in a frying pan over a low heat. Add the shallot, garlic, thyme, rosemary and bay leaf and sweat down (cook slowly without colour) for about 15 minutes. Remove from the heat and allow to cool down. This is a good time to set up your mincer (grinder) and to line your terrine mould.

Preheat the oven to 150°C (300°F).

Line the inside of a 10 × 30 cm (4 × 12 in) mould with heatproof plastic wrap, then with caul fat, backfat or streaky bacon. Make sure there is enough overhanging the sides, so you can tuck it over the top of the terrine when it is finished.

Mix the cooled sautéed shallot and herb mixture with the boned-out rabbit and the pork shoulder, then mince (grind) through a medium-sized blade (number 8 is good), into a stainless steel bowl. Add the parsley and white pepper and stir in well.

Weigh the mixture and add 1% of its weight in salt. For example, if the mixture weighs 1 kg (2 lb 3 oz), then you'll need 10 g (¼ oz) of salt. Mix the salt in very well, using your hand or a wooden spoon.

Take the lined terrine mould and spread the mixture across the base, about 1 cm (½ in) thick, then add a layer of the kidneys and backstraps. Continue this until all the mixture is used up. Tap the terrine mould on the bench to allow the contents to settle, then fold over the caul fat, backfat or bacon, followed by the plastic wrap and foil. If the mould has a lid, put it on; if not, wrap the top with foil, to help keep the moisture in.

Next, place the mould into a larger heatproof dish, fill the dish with water to come halfway up the side of the terrine, then put the whole thing into the oven.

After 60 minutes, check the terrine by removing the lid or foil and sticking a meat thermometer in. If the temperature registers over 72°C (160°F), the terrine is fine to remove from the oven and leave to cool down and rest with the lid on. With terrines, the slower the cooking, the better.

Once it is cool to the touch, place the terrine in the fridge to set overnight. To remove it from the mould, grab the plastic wrap at the sides and pull it out of the mould, then unwrap.

The terrine is best served in slices, with crusty bread and pickles (see page 209).

Duck rilettes & rabbit terrine

Confit quail

DUCK RILLETTES

I must've prepared a tonne of pork rillettes for my market stall in Tasmania over the ten years that I ran it. My kids grew up eating pork rillettes out of the jar with a spoon, or would hang off my leg in the kitchen tugging every time they wanted a handful to stuff in their faces as I was making the next batch. Before farming pigs, I always made my rillettes out of duck.

MAKES 300–400 G (10½–14 OZ)

2 black ducks – or any duck you can get
100 g (3½ oz) sea salt flakes
1 litre (34 fl oz/4 cups) duck fat
3 bay leaves
7 juniper berries, cracked
1 rosemary sprig
1 thyme sprig
1 tablespoon black peppercorns

Cut the ducks in half lengthways, then press down on the breastbone with your hands to make them as flat as possible. Place in a plastic container and rub the salt generously all over. Cover and refrigerate for 12 hours.

Remove the ducks from the fridge, rinse off the salt, then pat dry with paper towel. Place the ducks in a large deep saucepan, then add the duck fat, making sure the pan is deep enough to cover them.

Add the bay leaves, juniper berries, rosemary, thyme and peppercorns and bring to the boil, then reduce the temperature to a rolling simmer and cook for 4–6 hours. Check the meat with a fork – it should come away from the bone easily.

Pull the ducks out of the pot with a spider strainer or slotted spoon and place in a non-reactive bowl. Strain the liquid and set aside to cool down.

Once the ducks are cool, start to pick the meat away from the bones and skin, keeping the meat separate; the bones and skin can be discarded.

Take the bowl of duck meat and, with your hand, start to shred the meat until it is the consistency of tinned tuna. Once shredded, place the meat in a serving bowl and pour the cooled stock liquid on top.

You can serve the rillettes straight away, as they are best served at room temperature, with cornichons and crusty bread. Or, you can place them in the fridge to set overnight, and take them out of the fridge at least 2 hours before serving.

The rillettes will keep for at least 2 weeks in the fridge – but I doubt they will stay in there that long before being eaten.

‡ **NOTE**
You'll need to start this dish the day before.

RABBIT, GOOSE & DUCK PÂTÉ EN CROÛTE

To me, this is the pinnacle of French charcuterie. You are cooking a meat terrine in pastry, then setting jelly around the terrine inside that pastry. It takes skill, time and all of your patience to get a pâté en croûte perfect. Once you do, you will want to make it all the time.

If you don't have a terrine mould, you can use a bread tin or cake tin here. You'll want it to be about 30 cm (12 in) long, 9 cm (3½ in) wide and 7 cm (2¾ in) deep.

MAKES A 1.5 KG (3 LB 5 OZ) LOAF

1–2 portions Rabbit terrine (page 171)

2 goose breasts, skinned and sliced into strips

2 duck breasts, skinned and sliced into strips

PASTRY

175 g (6 oz) chilled butter, chopped

500 g (1 lb 2 oz/3⅓ cups) plain (all-purpose) flour

10 g (¼ oz) salt

JELLY

4 pig's trotters, split in half lengthways

1 brown onion, halved

2 garlic cloves, crushed

3 thyme sprigs

5 juniper berries

1 bay leaf

170 ml (5½ fl oz/⅔ cup) Marsala

Put the jelly ingredients in a stockpot or large saucepan, with enough water to cover the trotters. Bring to the boil, then reduce the heat to a low simmer and cook for 1–2 hours. Then turn the heat up to high and reduce the liquid by half, which will take about 15 minutes. Remove from the heat, strain out all the solids and set aside to cool.

Meanwhile, make the pastry. Put the butter, flour and salt in a food processor and pulse until the mixture has a sand-like texture (or you can mix by hand if you want). Heat 150 ml (5 fl oz) water to just under boiling point and add this to the pastry, then pulse or stir very quickly so no lumps form.

Turn the dough out onto a lightly floured bench. Knead for 2 minutes, or until it forms a ball with a slightly silky, smooth texture. Cover the dough with a damp towel and refrigerate for at least 1 hour.

Preheat the oven to 165°C (330°F).

Set aside one-fifth of the pastry for the lid. Roll out the remaining pastry, into a large rectangle, about 50 × 30 cm (19½ × 12 in), and 3 mm (⅛ in) thick. Gently lower the pastry into your terrine or bread tin, making sure it comes up each edge and overhangs by at least 2 cm (¾ in). Press the pastry down using a little pinched ball of pastry, making sure you get the pastry into every corner of the tin.

Press a 1 cm (½ in) layer of the rabbit into the bottom of the tin, then place a layer of goose and duck strips along the length of the tin. Add another layer of rabbit, then goose, then duck. Repeat until all the meat is used.

Grab the tin by the side and give it a good tap on the bench, to knock out any air bubbles, then press down firmly on the top layer.

Roll out the reserved pastry to make a rectangle large enough for the lid, then brush the edges with a little water and place it on the terrine. Use your fingers to crimp the pastry lid onto the overhanging pastry edges. Cut two flute holes, about 2.5 cm (1 in) in diameter, in the top of the pastry. Make a couple of foil chimneys and stick them into the flute holes, to stop the meat juices flowing out the top of the pie and running down the sides, which will cause the finished dish to stick to the mould.

Place the terrine in the oven in a roasting tin and bake for 70 minutes. Check to see if it is cooked by using a meat thermometer; 75°C (165°F) is the internal temperature you want.

Remove the pâté en croûte from the oven and let it cool in the terrine mould or tin for at least 2 hours.

Remove the pâté en croûte from the mould and set it on a clean bench. If the jelly has set, warm it slightly so it's at a pouring consistency, then pour the jelly down the pastry flutes, until it comes to the top.

Chill the pâté en croûte in the fridge for 20–30 minutes, then check to see if the jelly is up to the top of the pastry flutes. If it isn't, pour in some more jelly until it reaches the top again, and repeat this process until the jelly is all the way up to the top.

Now set the pâté en croûte in the fridge overnight; it will keep in your fridge for up to 2 weeks. To serve, simply cut and enjoy with good pickles and mustard.

DRY-CURE NITRATE-FREE BACON

I made this bacon weekly for many years for my market stall business, which seems a lifetime ago now. Being nitrate-free was a big selling point, as people are looking for food containing as few preservatives as possible. I did find some friends didn't like the taste of my bacon due to its lack of nitrate, as it is actually nitrate that gives bacon that generic flavour we all associate with bacon – but I prefer the way the nitrate-free version tastes and cooks. I used the whole mid-loin and hot-smoked it, as I found this gave a better shelf life, but I've written this recipe with the belly, as it can be used in other dishes in the book – and streaky bacon really is the best bacon in a sandwich.

MAKES ABOUT 1.5 KG (3 LB 5 OZ)

600 g (1 lb 5 oz) pure sea salt
300 g (10½ oz) white sugar
100 g (3½ oz) soft brown sugar
2 kg (4 lb 6 oz) whole piece of pork belly or scotch

In a large bowl, combine the salt and sugars. Add the pork and rub the mixture over and all around.

Sprinkle some of the salt mixture into a large non-reactive container that is big enough to fit the pork. Place the pork in the container, then cover with the remaining salt mixture. (If you don't have a container big enough, a zip-lock bag will do; if you have a food vacuum-packing machine or vacuum sealer, even better – simply seal the pork belly in with the salt mixture.)

Place the whole thing in the fridge and allow the belly to cure for 3–4 days in the fridge, making sure to turn the belly in the mixture every day; the mixture will become a slurry, which is nothing to be worried about. (If the pork is sealed in a bag, just turn the bag daily.)

After the pork is cured, remove it from the salt mixture and pat dry with paper towel.

Hot-smoke the belly (see page 15) until the internal temperature reaches 75°C (165°F) on a meat thermometer.

You can use the bacon immediately. If it doesn't get eaten straight away, it is best stored wrapped in wax paper in the fridge, and will last for 2–3 weeks.

OLD-SCHOOL COOKED HAM

This ham is made the traditional way, by curing, smoking and then boiling the pork. You can use this method with any game meat you desire. It works best with the back legs or 'haunch', but you can use the shoulder as well. You can also take this recipe as a base and change up the brine by adding booze and molasses for a different result.

MAKES 3 KG (6 LB 9 OZ)

3 kg (6 lb 9 oz) boneless pork leg

kitchen twine or meat netting/
    netting sock

CURING MIXTURE

3 litres (101 fl oz/12 cups) water

450 g (1 lb) pure sea salt

1 tablespoon Cure salt #1 (see
    page 165)

Take a large tub or bucket big enough to submerge the ham in. Add the curing mix ingredients, mixing until fully dissolved. Stab the pork with a paring knife, about six times on each side, to allow the cure to penetrate. Place the pork into the brine and make sure it's fully submerged – you may need to weigh it down with a plate.

Cover the tub with a lid; if it doesn't have a lid, I find a plate works well.

Place in the fridge and leave for 1½ days per 1 kg (2 lb 3 oz) of meat. A 3 kg (6 lb 9 oz) piece will take 4½ days.

Remove from the brine and tie the pork (see photo on left).

Place the cured pork in a large pot, cover with fresh water and bring to the boil. Set the water to a rolling simmer and cook the pork until the internal temperature reaches 80°C (175°F) on a meat thermometer. It should take about 2 hours to reach this temperature.

Remove the pork from the water. You can then either hot- or cold-smoke the pork, it's up to you; either way, the internal temperature must reach 75°C (165°F). Cold smoking will take up to 8 hours, and hot smoking around 3 hours.

Once it has been smoked, let the ham sit for at least 24 hours in the fridge before you slice it.

Once you slice into it, keep the ham wrapped in a tea towel in the fridge and it should keep for at least 4 weeks.

CAPOCOLLO

Capocollo is dry-cured pork – usually a whole pork scotch or neck. I have used this recipe for a few years, with a little change here or there along the way. I have also done a version using a sambar deer scotch fillet, and the result was off the charts. This is a great charcuterie item that fits on any meat platter. I'll even have it with some fresh broad (fava) beans tossed in extra virgin olive oil and lemon juice.

MAKES 2

2 whole pork scotch or neck fillets, about 1 kg (2 lb 3 oz) each

10 g (¼ oz) ground cloves

10 g (¼ oz) ground cinnamon

10 g (¼ oz) ground mace

15 g (½ oz) ground juniper berries

20 g (¾ oz) ground fennel seeds

20 g (¾ oz) ground white pepper

50 g (1¾ oz) pure sea salt (2.5% of the weight of the pork)

½ teaspoon Bactoferm (see page 165)

½ teaspoon Cure salt #1 (see page 165)

2 lengths of meat netting (see page 165)

lard, if necessary

Trim the pork fillets. Place each one in a non-reactive container or zip-lock bag. Equally divide all the spices, salt, Bactoferm and Cure salt #1 between the pork fillets and mix well.

Cover or seal, then refrigerate for 2 weeks, turning the pork every couple of days. The pork will be ready when it's firm to touch, as if the muscles are all stiff. If it takes longer, then so be it.

When you are ready to proceed, cut a length of meat netting 10 cm (4 in) longer than each pork fillet. Thread the netting over the pork by stretching it out over the pork and pulling it up like a sock. Once this is done, tie off each end with kitchen twine so it doesn't fall out when you hang it.

Hang the pork in your curing area, which should be about 12°C (53.5°F) or cooler, and humid; wine fridges are a great little item to do all your charcuterie in.

The capocollo should be ready in about 7–9 weeks. To check, slice one open – it should be cured all the way through, and have a stained-glass appearance. If it isn't cured, seal the end with some lard and hang it further until it is.

Once cured, it will keep for a least 3 months. You can slice it down and seal the slices separately, or keep the capocollo whole, wrapped in a tea towel or muslin (cheesecloth) in the fridge, and slice it as you go.

PROSCIUTTO

I have this mate Matthew (a.k.a. 'The Gourmet Farmer'). We had an artisanal farm food business together for a few years, and even kept in contact when we dissolved it. From the start, Matthew had an obsession with making prosciutto. So, I have stolen his recipe, as I know how much effort he would have put into it. I find that with game meat, the prosciutto can become a little too dry, but for backpack hunts it's light and a great source of protein. As with the ham recipe on page 179, you can try this with any game meat.

MAKES 3 KG (6 LB 9 OZ)

5 kg (11 lb) pork leg, bone in

2 kg (4 lb 6 oz) table sea salt

lard, for smearing

coarsely ground black pepper

fly netting or fine cloth such as muslin (cheesecloth), to protect against insects

a swag of patience

Trim the pork leg well, so it doesn't have any little bits of meat hanging off, or deep cuts. Trim it, so it is rounded at the base.

To soften the meat, I give it a decent walloping with a wooden rolling pin for about 30–40 whacks, trying to give all the leg a bit of a seeing-to, avoiding the bone.

There is likely to be some blood in an artery that runs down the leg, and you can squeeze this out by pressing from the foot end, up along the bone and towards the hip joint. Only a teaspoon or less will be there, and I mop it up using paper towel. Some people inject the artery with a brine solution from the foot end, to flush it out, but I find that hard to do, and the pressing method is just as successful.

Take a large non-reactive tub, preferably one with a lid, and put some of the salt in the bottom. Place the leg in the tub and rub the salt liberally all over, particularly around the exposed ball joint area. Lay the leg, whole side down, on a bed of salt and cover the exposed meat with more salt. Place a weight on top of the leg; about 5–8 kg (11–17½ lb) of weight is good. You could use a flour bag or water containers, making sure you first cover the leg with plastic wrap to protect it against the weight.

Keep the leg in the salt for about 10 days at 12°C (53.5°F) or below; allow 1½–2 days per 1 kg (2 lb 3 oz). During this time, every second day, keep turning the pork and rubbing the slurry of salt over it.

When the leg has cured, remove it from the salt and wash it off. Many people rub red wine vinegar over the pork at this point to keep the surface sterile.

Smear the leg with enough lard to completely seal it. Scatter coarsely ground black pepper over the lard, which helps with keeping insects away.

Hang the leg in a cool place, at 12°C (53.5°F) or below – you want cool and humid, rather than a cool room, which is cold and dry. In some areas, you may need to cover the meat with fly netting to keep insects off.

Hang the meat for at least 6 months before you cut into the leg or try to eat it. This will be long enough for the curing process to do its job – but 1 year of hanging would be even better. Ideally, it will get a bloom of white mould all over it after a few weeks. This is fine and part of the process; if you are bothered by it, you can wipe the leg down with a clean cloth to remove it.

When the prosciutto is ready to eat, scrub off the mould and the lard, perhaps trimming the outside meat as well.

Store the leg wrapped in a tea towel, either in the fridge or in a larder. It will dry out more quickly in the larder, so if you are not eating it fast enough, putting it in the fridge will slow down the drying process. I have had legs hang for 3 years, which I have then eaten over a 4 month period.

Cut very fine slices of the ham and serve simply, perhaps with fragrant melon, grissini or sweet summer figs.

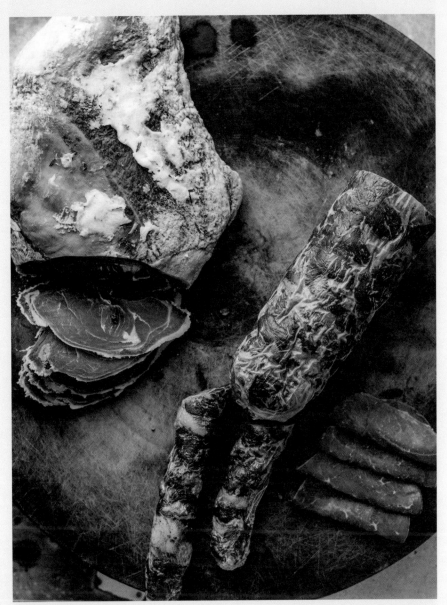

Cured deliciousness

WALLABY PASTRAMI

I never ate much kangaroo or wallaby until I moved to Tasmania. Now, since moving to rural Victoria, it's what I miss the most. Traditionally, pastrami is made with beef, but I find wallaby meat has a real sweetness that comes out in the smoker. You can also make this with venison to get a great result.

MAKES 1.5 KG (3 LB 5 OZ)

2 kg (4 lb 6 oz) wallaby topside
  (or a whole boned-out haunch)
2 tablespoons ground black pepper
2 tablespoons ground coriander

BRINE
200 g (7 oz) pure sea salt
150 g (5½ oz) soft brown sugar
3 garlic cloves, crushed
1 tablespoon brown mustard seeds
1 tablespoon ground allspice
1 tablespoon ground mace
1 teaspoon chilli flakes (optional)

Heat your smoker to 120°C (250°F).

Combine all the brine ingredients in a large pot, add 2 litres (68 fl oz/8 cups) water and bring up to the boil. Once the salt and sugar have dissolved, remove from the heat and allow to cool down.

Place the wallaby in a clean bucket and cover with the cold brine. Place a plate or weight of some kind on top to keep the wallaby fully submerged. Cover the bucket with a lid. Refrigerate for 3 days.

Remove the wallaby from the brine, pat dry with a tea towel and place it on a tray. Rub the wallaby with black pepper and coriander, making sure you get them all over, then place the wallaby into your smoker.

Smoke the wallaby for 1–2 hours, or until the internal temperature reaches 72°C (160°F) on a meat thermometer. Once you have reached the desired temperature, remove the pastrami from the smoker and let it rest for at least 30 minutes before you slice it.

You can eat this hot from the smoker, or let it cool down for cold cuts. Being corned, it will keep for a few weeks in your fridge in a sealed airtight container.

KANGAROO LOMO

As with many things, a lot of dishes do get a little lost in translation. *Lomo* is simply the Spanish term for 'loin' – but it most often refers to an air-cured loin of pork. I have always done most of my charcuterie using meat from pigs, but this simple air-dried recipe is also great with kangaroo loin, which gives a surprisingly similar result. Native pepper berries add an extra dimension to the flavour.

MAKES 6

2 tablespoons Australian native pepper berries (or use a mix of black peppercorns and juniper berries)

300 g (10½ oz) pure sea salt

6 kangaroo loins

lard (optional)

Using a spice grinder, finely grind the pepper berries with 1 tablespoon of the salt, then mix it with the rest of the salt.

Sprinkle half the mixture into a non-reactive container and place the kangaroo loins on top. Cover the kangaroo with the rest of the salt and pepper berry mix, rubbing it in.

Leave the container in the fridge for 2–3 days.

Remove from the fridge, rinse off the curing salt and pat dry with a tea towel. Rub the kangaroo with a little lard to stop it drying out too quickly, or wrap it in muslin (cheesecloth).

Place the loins in your curing area to dry out. Your curing area should be around 12°C (53.5°F) or cooler, and humid; wine fridges are a great little item to do all your charcuterie in.

The lomo should be ready in about 6 weeks. Check it by slicing an end off to see if it has cured all the way through to the middle. If it hasn't, hang the loins a little longer.

The lomo is best stored wrapped in wax paper in the fridge, and will last for up to 6 weeks.

Wallaby pastrami

HUNTER'S SAUSAGES

Traditional hunter's sausage is from Poland and made with pork. My idea of a hunter's sausage is a bit different in that I use whatever game I have harvested. The spices are always the same, and I use the smallest sausage casings I can get, so the sausages dry out well and will keep in my pack when out in the bush.

MAKES 25–30 THIN SAUSAGE STICKS

1 runner of sheep sausage casings, 24–26 mm (1 in) in diameter

800 g (1 lb 12 oz) beef (trimmings are fine)

800 g (1 lb 12 oz) venison (trimmings are fine)

400 g (14 oz) beef or pork fat (whatever you can get)

60 g (2 oz) sweet paprika

10 g (¼ oz) mustard powder

10 g (¼ oz) ground white pepper

10 g (¼ oz) celery salt

10 g (¼ oz) garlic powder

10 g (¼ oz) ground mace

pure sea salt (2% of the overall weight of the sausage mixture)

a pinch of Cure salt #1 (see page 165)

¼ teaspoon Bactoferm (see page 165)

Soak the sausage casings in water for 1 hour.

Grind the beef, venison and fat using a medium-sized (#8–10) mincing plate, into a sterilised bowl or container. Mix in the spices.

Weigh the mixture and add 2% of its weight in salt. For example, if the mixture weighs 2 kg (4 lb 6 oz), then you'll need 40 g (1½ oz) of salt.

Mix in the salt, Cure salt #1 and Bactoferm, then mince (grind) the mixture through the same plate.

Fill the bowl of your sausage cannon with the mixture. Thread the sausage casings onto the nozzle and start to pump (see page 166).

Once you have the sausages done and tied, let them hang for 30 minutes while you heat your smoker to 55°C (130°F).

Put the sausages in the smoker and increase the temperature to 75°C (165°F). Cook until the internal temperature of the sausages reaches 65°C (150°F) on a meat thermometer; this should take around 1 hour.

Remove the sausages from the smoker and cool them down in an ice bath straight away. Once they have cooled down, which will take about 20 minutes, store them in the fridge.

The sausages will have an approximate shelf life of 2 weeks, and you can take them backpacking in the colder months.

‡ NOTE

See pages 164–167 for tips on sausage preparation and pumping.

VENISON SAUCISSON SEC

Saucisson sec is a simple air-dried sausage that translates from French as 'dried sausage'. For an air-dried sausage, I like to include pork cuts that run at 20–25% fat. That way you don't need to add extra fat (unlike the fresh venison sausages on page 196, which use lamb trimmings), and I find the flavour of a complete muscle better than straight fat. I suppose having farmed old-breed pigs for ten years may have a bit to do with it.

MAKES 7–9 SAUSAGES

1 runner of sausage casings, 32–35 mm (1¼–1½ in) in diameter

1.5 kg (3 lb 5 oz) venison meat – I use all the offcuts from the prime cuts

500 g (1 lb 2 oz) fatty pork scotch fillet or pork belly

5 garlic cloves, crushed

40 g (1½ oz) pure sea salt

40 g (1½ oz) ground black pepper

a good pinch of Bactoferm (see page 165)

a good pinch of Cure salt #1 (see page 165)

Soak the sausage casings in water for 1 hour.

Mince (grind) the venison and pork using a medium size (#8–10) mincing (grinding) plate, into a sterilised bowl or container. Mix in the garlic, salt, pepper, Bactoferm and Cure #1.

Fill the bowl of the sausage cannon with the mixture. Thread the sausage casings onto the nozzle and start to pump (see page 166).

Once you have the sausages done and tied, let them hang for a few hours before you put them in your curing area. Your curing area should be around 12°C (53.5°F) or cooler, and humid; wine fridges are a great little item to do all your charcuterie in.

After the first day of drying, prick the sausages all over with your salami pricker or a fine needle. This helps get some air through to the centre of the sausages, to help them breathe and cure.

The sausages should be ready in about 4–6 weeks. Slice the end off one to see if it has cured all the way through. If they are a little soft in the middle, you can slice and grill them at any time.

Once fully cured, the sausages will keep in the fridge for a couple of months – but do vacuum-pack them if you can, to stop them drying out too much.

‡ **NOTE**
See pages 164–167 for tips on sausage preparation and pumping.

BUFFALO-HEART MORTADELLA

I have made mortadella a few times with a mate, Mic Giuliani (a.k.a. Cannoli), based on an old family recipe of his. We'd just grind the meat using a mincer, and then bind the mixture with gelatine and milk powder, which worked just fine. After making frankfurters for a while, I got better at emulsifying on a small scale, which I find works better when using heart as the main meat. I have scaled down the recipe to only make two sausages, so you can use a home food processor – but you'll need the biggest food processor you can get your hands on.

MAKES 2 SAUSAGES

2 sheep bung sausage casings (see page 165)

800 g (1 lb 12 oz) trimmed buffalo heart

300 g (10½ oz) pork fat

25 g (1 oz) pure sea salt (2% of the overall weight of the buffalo heart and pork mixture)

1 teaspoon ground black pepper

10 g (¼ oz) ground mace

10 g (¼ oz) ground coriander

5 g (⅛ oz) ground allspice

a pinch of Cure salt #1 (see page 165)

shaved ice, for emulsifying

GARNISHES

40 g (1½ oz) pitted green olives, split

50 g (1¾ oz) pork fat, diced

Soak the sausage casings in water for 1 hour.

Mince (grind) the buffalo heart using a medium-sized (#8–10) mincing (grinding) plate, into a sterilised bowl or container. Weigh the mixture, then cover with baking paper and place in the fridge to keep cool.

Now mince the pork fat through the same mincing blade. Place on top of the buffalo heart and place in the fridge to keep cool.

Set up your food processor, then add the buffalo heart, pork fat, salt, pepper, ground spices and Cure salt #1, then turn the machine on. At this stage you don't want the meat mixture to get hot, as it will split and won't bind properly. You want to keep it under 25°C (77°F) – so this is where the shaved ice comes in. You want to blend the heart mixture until it lightens in colour and fluffs up; this should take a few minutes, and you may have to stop the processor and push the mixture back down. Every 40 seconds, put a tablespoon or two of shaved ice in to help with this process.

Remove the mixture and place in a bowl, setting it over another bowl with ice in it. Fold in the garnishes and you are ready to pump.

While you are setting up your sausage machine and skins, place the mixture in the fridge or freezer.

Fill the bowl of the sausage cannon with the mixture. Thread the sausage casings onto the nozzle and start to pump (see page 166).

Once you have the sausages done and tied, let them hang for 30 minutes while you heat your smoker to 55°C (130°F).

Put the sausages in the smoker and increase the temperature to 75°C (165°F). Cook until the internal temperature of the mortadella reaches 65°C (150°F) on a meat thermometer. This could take anywhere from 1–3 hours. (If you don't have a smoker, you can steam or poach the sausages until the same internal temperature – 65°C/150°F – is reached. They won't have the same flavour as the smoked sausages, but will still taste great.)

Remove the sausages from the smoker (or steamer/poacher) and cool them down in an ice bath straight away. Once they have cooled down, which will take about 20 minutes, store them in the fridge.

It's best to let the sausages set overnight before eating, so they don't tear or rip as you slice into them, but if you can't wait, you can eat them as soon as they've been fully cooked.

Whole or sliced, the mortadella will keep for about 2 weeks in the fridge in an airtight container.

‡ NOTE
See pages 164–167 for tips on sausage preparation and pumping.

PORK & FENNEL SAUSAGES

These sausages are a go-to in my book. I have made kilos and kilos of them over the years. You might think that the fennel seeds will overpower the flavour, but mixed with the pork they seem to sing together.

MAKES 3 KG (6 LB 10 OZ) OF SAUSAGE MIXTURE,
OR 36 SAUSAGES

1 runner of sausage casings,
    28–32 mm (1¼–1½ in) in diameter

3 kg (6 lb 10 oz) pork shoulder

30 g (1 oz) pure sea salt
    (1% of the weight of the pork)

1 teaspoon ground black pepper

1 teaspoon fennel seeds

Soak the sausage casings in water for 1 hour.

Mince (grind) the pork using a medium-sized (#8–10) mincing (grinding)plate, into a sterilised bowl or container.

Mix in the salt, pepper and fennel seeds.

Fill the bowl of the sausage cannon with the mixture. Thread the sausage casings onto the nozzle and start to pump (see page 166).

Once you have the sausages done and tied, let them hang for at least 3 hours – but no longer than 12 hours – before you cook them.

‡ NOTE
See pages 164–167 for tips on sausage preparation and pumping.

PORK, PAPRIKA & FENNEL CACCIATORE SAUSAGES

It's just a few extra steps from the fresh pork and fennel sausages (opposite) to this air-dried Italian classic. Another great protein to throw in your pack on the long trips.

MAKES 3 KG (6 LB 10 OZ) OF SAUSAGE MIXTURE, OR 36 SAUSAGES

1 runner of sausage casings, 28–32 mm (1¼–1½ in) in diameter

3 kg (6 lb 9 oz) pork shoulder

75 g (2¾ oz) pure sea salt (2.5% of the weight of the pork)

50 g (1¾ oz) sweet paprika

1 teaspoon ground black pepper

1 teaspoon fennel seeds

1 teaspoon Cure salt #1 (see page 165)

Soak the sausage casings in water for 1 hour.

Mince (grind) the pork using a medium-sized (#8–10) mincing (grinding) plate, into a sterilised bowl or container.

Mix in the salt, paprika, pepper, fennel seeds and Cure salt #1.

Fill the bowl of the sausage cannon with the mixture. Thread the sausage casings onto the nozzle and start to pump (see page 166).

Once you have the sausages done and tied, let them hang for a few hours before you put them in your curing area. Your curing area should be around 12°C (53.5°F) or cooler, and humid; wine fridges are a great little item to do all your charcuterie in.

After the first day of drying, prick all the sausages with a salami pricker, to help them breathe.

They should be fully cured in about 4 weeks.

To check them, cut off one end of a sausage and inspect to see if it has cured all the way to the centre. You want them firm all the way to the middle, or they won't be safe to eat raw. If you cut them and they're a little soft in the middle, you can still grill them and then eat them, so you are not wasting a sausage.

‡ **NOTE**
See pages 164–167 for tips on sausage preparation and pumping.

CEVAPCICI

I do love a sausage (or as I like to call them, a 'Rossage'). This would have to be one of my favourite sausages of all time – and it is skinless! *Cevapcici* originally hail from the Balkans – and this recipe even met the approval of a friend's Croatian wife. It cooks up just perfectly over hot coals. It is best made and cooked on the same day, as the sausages oxidise very quickly, having no casing. I find the cold cooked cevapcici a ripper of a snack the next day.

MAKES 30

500 g (1 lb 2 oz) minced (ground) venison

300 g (10½ oz) minced (ground) pork

200 g (7 oz) minced (ground) goat

1 free-range egg white

4 garlic cloves, crushed

½ teaspoon bicarbonate soda (baking soda)

3 tablespoons sweet paprika

½ teaspoon cayenne pepper (optional)

1 tablespoon pure sea salt

2 tablespoons ground black pepper

Wash and sanitise your hands. (Some people prefer to use disposable gloves, but I think you can lose the feel of what you are doing, and with sausage-making that is important.)

Combine all of the ingredients until the mixture has a paste-like texture. You can achieve this by giving it a really good mix with your hands and squishing it as much as possible, then working your hands like a paddle, which helps the proteins bind. But you can also use a standing electric mixer fitted with the paddle attachment, and do it in batches.

Take a clean piping (icing) bag, without a nozzle attachment. Fill it with the meat mixture and slowly push the mixture out the end, to make sausages about 7–9 cm (2¾–3½ in) long. Alternatively, you could use a sausage cannon.

The sausages are ready to cook straight away; they will need about 5–7 minutes each side. I love these as a breakfast sausage with bread and butter.

194

STAG SNAGS

I have made and sold hundreds of kilos of fresh sausages in my time. This recipe is so simple, but I think it really captures the flavour and texture of venison. It took me quite a few years to get it just right. I find lamb belly trimmings the best meat to mix with venison for a fresh sausage.

MAKES 30

1 runner of sausage casings,
    32–35 mm (1¼–1½ in) in diameter

2.5 kg (5½ lb) venison meat –
    I use all the offcuts from the
    prime cuts

500 g (1 lb 2 oz) lamb trimmings

30 g (1 oz) pure sea salt
    (1% of the overall meat weight)

1 teaspoon ground white pepper

a good pinch of ground mace

Soak the sausage casings in water for 1 hour.

Mince (grind) the venison and lamb using a medium-sized (#8–10) mincing (grinding) plate, into a sterilised bowl or container. Mix in the salt, pepper and mace, then mince again using the same plate.

Fill the bowl of the sausage cannon with the mixture. Thread the sausage casings onto the nozzle and start to pump (see page 166).

Once you have the sausages done and tied, let them hang for at least 3 hours before you cook them. If you can hang them overnight, they will set better, but I would let a fresh sausage hang no longer than 12 hours.

‡ NOTE
    See pages 164–167 for tips on sausage preparation
    and pumping.

POSSUM KRANSKY

The Carniolan sausage, like many dishes, came from the corners of Europe to the shores of Australia. We then mass-produced it and renamed it kransky. It is traditionally made with pork, but this version uses possum, as I find its subtle flavour mixes really well with pork and bacon. A hunter I knew used to do a cheese version using wallaby and possum, and they were tasty, so you can add some cheddar to these ones too, if you like. And if you're not up for making sausages, just leave out the Bactoferm and Cure salt #1 and turn the mixture into rissoles, a meatloaf or even a bolognese sauce instead.

MAKES 3 KG (6 LB 10 OZ) OF KRANSKY MIXTURE,
OR 40 SAUSAGES

1 runner of sausage casings,
    28–32 mm (1–1¼ in) in diameter

1.5 kg (3 lb 5 oz) possum meat,
    cut into chunks

1 kg (2 lb 3 oz) pork meat,
    cut into chunks

500 g (1 lb 2 oz) belly bacon
    (page 176), cut into chunks

125 ml (4 fl oz/½ cup) white wine

125 g (4½ oz) cheddar (optional),
    roughly grated

50 g (1¾ oz) rice flour

3 garlic cloves, roughly chopped

1 teaspoon ground black pepper

30 g (1 oz) pure sea salt (1% of
    the overall weight of the
    sausage mixture)

a pinch of Bactoferm (see page 165)

a pinch of Cure salt #1 (see page 165)

Soak the sausage casings in water for 1 hour.

Mince (grind) the possum, pork and bacon using a medium-sized (#8–10) mincing (grinding) plate, into a sterilised bowl or container. Mix in the remaining ingredients.

Now mince the whole mixture again, through the same plate.

Fill the bowl of the sausage cannon with the mixture. Thread the sausage casings onto the nozzle and start to pump (see page 166).

Once you have the sausages done and tied, let them hang for 30 minutes while you heat your smoker to 55°C (130°F).

Start to smoke the sausages and increase the temperature to 75°C (165°F). Cook for about 1½ hours, or until the internal temperature of the sausages reaches 65°C (150°F) when tested with a meat thermometer.

Remove the sausages from the smoker and cool in an ice bath straight away, which will take about 20 minutes, then store in the fridge.

They will keep in the fridge for about 2 weeks, or longer if vacuum-packed, and you can take them backpacking in the colder months.

‡ **NOTE**
  **See pages 164–167 for tips on sausage preparation
  and pumping.**

N.08

LARDER

Condiments are a great way to add instant flavour and enhance a meal. I have never really been a person who smothers a dinner in gravy, but I have always loved a good mustard, horseradish and hot sauce – and nothing beats a home-made sauce, relish or rub. Here are a few recipes for condiments that you can store in your larder and enjoy all year round. Use the recipes as they are, or as a base to create your own.

MY MUSTARD

When I had my business Bruny Island Food, it was all based around our hand-raised pigs, turned into charcuterie products. I did also branch off into a few sidelines, including selling my own mustard, which had a bit of a cult following. I'm not much of a gravy person, so mustard is my go-to with any meat. A good mix between a French and German mustard, this one is based on a dijon style, but hotter – and the longer it sits, the better it gets.

MAKES ABOUT 2 KG (4 LB 6 OZ/8 CUPS)

1 kg (2 lb 3 oz) mustard flour (from spice shops and Asian grocers – not to be confused with mustard powder)

1.15 litres (39 fl oz) cold water

1.5 litres (51 fl oz/6 cups) white wine vinegar

1.5 litres (51 fl oz/6 cups) verjuice

3 brown onions, sliced

5 garlic cloves, crushed

2 bay leaves

1 tablespoon whole black peppercorns

1 tablespoon juniper berries

100 g (3½ oz) salt

60 g (2 oz) sugar

juice of 2 lemons

In a large bowl, combine the mustard flour and water to make a paste. Set aside.

In a large saucepan or stockpot, combine the vinegar, verjuice, onion, garlic, bay leaves, peppercorns and juniper berries. Bring to the boil over a high heat, then turn the heat down to a rolling simmer. Cook for about 30–40 minutes, until the liquid reduces by two-thirds. Strain the mixture and leave to cool.

Stir the cooled vinegar reduction into the mustard paste. Add the salt, sugar and lemon juice, then let the mixture stand for 20 minutes. (I don't know why letting the mixture sit at this point makes the mustard taste better – but it works!)

Transfer to a saucepan and warm up the mustard over a medium–low heat, just enough to get it to a simmer, then let it gently cook out for 5–10 minutes.

Remove from the heat and let cool slightly before bottling the mixture into clean jars.

The mustard will keep for a least a year in a cool dark place, but refrigerate after opening. I have never had this mustard go off, and I've had open jars in the fridge for 2 years.

SAMBAL

With my kids, I can't put chilli in anything – they just won't eat it. So I have loads of different chill sauces and pastes on the side, to keep my hot food intake up. This chilli sambal is from my time living in Indonesia, where it's a staple table item, dished around like we do tomato sauce.

MAKES 12 × 220 ML (7½ FL OZ) JARS

1 kg (2 lb 3 oz) long red chillies, topped

500 g (1 lb 2 oz) nice ripe tomatoes, cored and cut into quarters

75 ml (2½ fl oz) vegetable oil

180 ml (6 fl oz) fish sauce

350 g (12½ oz) palm sugar (jaggery), smashed

Working in batches, place the chillies and tomatoes in a blender and process into a fine paste. As you are reaching the fine paste stage, slowly drizzle in some of the oil to emulsify the mixture, distributing the oil among each batch. (If you don't do this, it won't keep its vibrant red colour after being cooked out in the next step.)

Pour the mixture into a stockpot or large saucepan. Stir in the fish sauce and palm sugar. Bring to the boil over a high heat, then turn the heat down to a slow simmer and let the mixture cook out, stirring constantly so it doesn't stick to the bottom of the pan. The sambal will be ready once all the excess juice is cooked away and it forms a paste-like texture. This should take 20–30 minutes.

Let the mixture cool slightly before bottling in clean jars.

The sambal will keep for a least a year in a cool dark place, but do refrigerate after opening. I don't know how long these will last opened in the fridge, because at my place the sambal is always gobbled up within a few weeks!

Nick's super seasoner, mustard & pickles

Tomato & BBQ sauce

NICK'S SUPER SEASONER (FERMENTED CHILLI SAUCE)

When I had my market stall, I thought I had it tough for all the work I did every week to get to 'sale day'. But my mate Nick Cummins made me look like a slouch. So I found it really surprising when I bought his 'super seasoner' one day and told him how much I liked it, and asked would he give me the recipe – and he handed it over without flinching, unlike most chefs or condiment producers. The recipe makes about 2.5 litres, which I know sounds like a lot – but it keeps pretty much forever and only gets better with age. It does take a week or so to ferment, so it's worth making a big batch of it.

MAKES 2.5 LITRES (85 FL OZ/10 CUPS)

100 g (3½ oz) garlic paste

300 ml (10 fl oz) water

250 ml (8½ fl oz/1 cup) white vinegar

250 ml (8½ fl oz/1 cup) rice wine vinegar

250 ml (8½ fl oz/1 cup) soy sauce

180 ml (6 fl oz) fish sauce

180 g (6½ oz) tomato paste (concentrated purée)

250 g (9 oz) minced chilli (from a jar)

FOR THE FERMENT

1 kg (2 lb 3 oz) long red chillies, topped

75 g (2½ oz) brown sugar

25 g (1 oz) salt

300 ml (10 fl oz) water

Place all the ingredients for the ferment in a blender and blitz to a fine paste. Transfer the paste to a fermenting crock or clean glass jar. Place a lid on top, but don't seal it, as there will be pressure building up.

Each day for the next 5 days, remove the top and stir the chilli mixture, to release the gases and to ensure it ferments evenly. Then replace the lid again, not sealing.

After 6 days pour the fermented chilli into a saucepan or stockpot, add the remaining ingredients and bring to the boil over a high heat. Turn the heat down to a rolling simmer and cook for 5 minutes, then remove from the heat.

Let the sauce cool a little bit before bottling in clean jars.

The sauce will separate when it sits in the fridge or cupboard, so give it a good shake before using. It only gets better with age – either sealed in the cupboard, or opened in the fridge.

TOMATO & BBQ SAUCE

For a while, the tomato sauce competition among my friends was getting out of control. Everyone was claiming their recipe as the best, being from their great-great-grandparents and so on; I think I even did a TV episode where this was one of the main topics.

So, I have completely ignored their recipes and made one of my own. I have grouped these two recipes together, as you use the tomato sauce base to make your barbecue sauce.

These sauces should keep well for at least a year in your pantry, and once opened, a few months in the fridge.

MAKES 3 LITRES (101 FL OZ/12 CUPS)

TOMATO SAUCE

2 kg (4 lb 6 oz) tomatoes, cored and seeded

3 brown onions, diced

3 green apples, cored and diced

5 garlic cloves, crushed

1 tablespoon ground cloves

1 tablespoon ground ginger

1 tablespoon ground allspice

1 tablespoon ground white pepper

50 g (1¾ oz) salt

50 ml (1¾ fl oz) malt vinegar

300 g (10½ oz) sugar

BARBECUE SAUCE

1 litre (34 fl oz/4 cups) Tomato sauce (from above)

250 ml (8½ fl oz/1 cup) apple cider vinegar

125 g (4½ oz) soft brown sugar

juice of 2 lemons

1 tablespoon Worcestershire sauce (page 206)

1 tablespoon Mustard (page 200)

1 tablespoon Dry rub (page 209)

a good splash of Fermented chilli sauce (opposite)

To make the tomato sauce, place the tomatoes, onion, apple, garlic, spices and salt in a stockpot or large saucepan, then bring to the boil over a high heat. Turn the heat down to a rolling simmer and cook for at least 40 minutes; make sure you keep stirring the mixture so it doesn't stick to the bottom of the pan. Once the onion and apple are soft, let the mixture cool a little, then pour it into a blender and blitz into a smooth sauce.

Tip the sauce back into the pot. Stir in the vinegar and sugar and cook over a low heat for 15 minutes. Remove from the heat and let your tomato sauce cool slightly before bottling in clean jars.

To make the barbecue sauce, combine all the ingredients in a large saucepan. Place over a low heat and leave to cook out for 15–20 minutes.

Remove from the heat and let the sauce cool a little before bottling in clean jars.

GREEN SAUCE (SALSA VERDE)

To me, green sauce is a must in any kitchen pantry. I love its versatility with game meat, turning a simple grilled piece of meat into a complete dish.

MAKES 500 ML (17 FL OZ/2 CUPS)

100 g (3½ oz) basil, picked

100 g (3½ oz) flat-leaf (Italian) parsley, picked

100 g (3½ oz) spring onions (scallions), roughly chopped

50 g (1¾ oz) chives, roughly chopped

3 garlic cloves, peeled

3 teaspoons baby capers, rinsed

5 anchovy fillets

juice of 2 lemons

200 ml (7 fl oz) extra virgin olive oil

Place all the ingredients in a food processor or blender and whiz until you have a paste. Check the seasoning for salt and pepper.

I guarantee the sauce will be used before it goes off, but to keep it fresh just make sure there is always oil covering the top of the paste.

It will keep in the fridge for up to 3 weeks.

WORCESTERSHIRE SAUCE

I used to buy Worcestershire sauce from the supermarket until I moved to Tasmania. Then I was buying it from friends. Now I finally make it myself. As with all recipes, there are so many different versions, but this is what I found to give the result I want.

MAKES 1 LITRE (34 FL OZ/4 CUPS)

4 garlic cloves, peeled

4 anchovy fillets

1 brown onion, peeled and quartered

1 litre (34 fl oz/4 cups) apple cider vinegar

250 ml (8½ fl oz/1 cup) molasses

100 g (3½ oz) soft brown sugar

250 ml (8½ fl oz/1 cup) soy sauce

60 g (2 oz) tamarind pulp

2 tablespoons ground allspice

1 long red chilli, split

1 tablespoon ground black pepper

½ teaspoon ground cloves

½ teaspoon ground ginger

Place the garlic, anchovies and onion in a food processor or blender and blitz into a fine paste.

Scrape the paste into a saucepan or stockpot, add all the other ingredients and bring to the boil. Once boiling, reduce the heat to a rolling simmer and let the mixture cook out for 30 minutes.

Leave to cool. Remove the chilli before bottling in clean jars.

Keep the sauce in your cupboard for at least 4 weeks before using. It will last there for a year, unopened. Once opened, keep it in the fridge and use within 3 months.

PRESERVED HORSERADISH

Fresh horseradish is one of the simple pleasures
in life. I always grow some in my garden and watch it
take over everything. It's easy to plant, but it's a great
idea to grow it in a pot or something that will contain
it. I have always grown it in old rainwater tanks.

MAKES 300 G (10½ OZ)

300 g (10½ oz) fresh horseradish root
1 tablespoon white wine vinegar
½ teaspoon salt

Peel the horseradish, then cut it into 3 cm (1¼ in) long
pieces. Place in a food processor and blend to a
fine paste.

Add the vinegar and salt and pulse the processor
to combine them through the horseradish.

Store in a clean jar or container in the fridge. You
can use it straight away, and it will keep its flavour for
at least 8 months.

CHIMICHURRI

South Americans really know how to barbecue meat –
and next to any barbecued meat is chimichurri.
To quote Anthony Bourdain, 'Chimichurri is to
Argentineans what ketchup is to North Americans'.

SERVES 10

125 ml (4 fl oz/½ cup) olive oil
30 ml (1 fl oz) red wine vinegar
1 bunch of flat-leaf (Italian)
    parsley, chopped
4 garlic cloves, crushed
2 red long red chillies,
    seeded and finely chopped
1 teaspoon sea salt flakes
ground black pepper, to taste

Combine all the ingredients in a bowl. Leave to sit
for at least 30 minutes to infuse before serving.

Any leftovers can be kept in the fridge for up
to a week, until the chimichurri loses its colour.

Horseradish, dry rub & chimichurri

DRY RUB

Everyone has their own recipe for a barbecue dry rub. This is the one I use, as I find it goes with any type of meat. I have adapted it from a pulled pork recipe, which I got from neighbours who lived in America. Like all the other recipes in this book, use this as a base and chop and change to suit your tastes.

MAKES ABOUT 500 G (1 LB 2 OZ)

100 g (3½ oz) sweet paprika
50 g (1¾ oz) mixed dried herbs
30 g (1 oz) garlic salt
50 g (1¾ oz) onion salt
50 g (1¾ oz) celery salt
50 g (1¾ oz) ground fennel seeds
50 g (1¾ oz) ground cumin
50 g (1¾ oz) ground coriander
20 g (¾ oz) ground black pepper
1 tablespoon chilli flakes
1 teaspoon ground mace

Combine all the spices in a bowl and give them a good mix.

Store in clean screw-top jars or a sealed container to keep fresh. The spices will start to lose their punch after a few months.

PICKLED CUCUMBERS

I have always loved pickled cucumbers, and love growing cucumbers in my garden for my yearly batch of pickles. The only problem is that I seem to run out every year before I am ready to make them again – so now I make big jars. This recipe is for one big jar. If you want to make extra, just time it for when the cucumber season is in full swing.

MAKES 1 KG (2 LB 3 OZ)

20 pickling cucumbers (see note), washed
500 ml (17 fl oz/2 cups) white wine vinegar
200 ml (7 fl oz) water
3 garlic cloves, sliced
2 French shallots, sliced
1 teaspoon brown mustard seeds
1 handful of wild fennel fronds
20 g (¾ oz) sea salt
1 teaspoon black peppercorns

Sterilise your jar and make sure the jar is warm, as you don't want it to crack when you pour the hot liquid in. Place the cucumbers in the jar.

Put all the other ingredients in a saucepan and bring to the boil, then take it off the heat and let the liquid cool slightly.

Pour the still-hot liquid into the jar, over the cucumbers. Seal the jar and leave it on the bench to cool down.

Once cooled, store in a dry dark cupboard for 8 weeks before opening. It will keep in the pantry for up to a year.

Refrigerate after opening and use within 3 months.

‡ NOTE
Pickling cucumbers are available from any place that sells seeds or seedlings. The pickling variety has a thinner skin and smaller seeds, but you have to watch them and pick them at the size you want. I have left some too long, and ended up with some cucumbers that are too big for the batches I am making.

GAME STOCK

A good stock is the base of all good cooking. Starting with a good base means you start with flavour, so you don't need to overcomplicate things to achieve a great dish. This is a basic stock that will help you utilise more of the animal you have harvested. The good thing about meat stock is that you only make it to the amount of bones you have, adding just enough water to cover the top of the bones.

MAKES 4 LITRES (135 FL OZ/16 CUPS)

4 kg (8 lb 13 oz) game bones

1 brown onion, roughly chopped

1 leek, white part only, roughly chopped

3 carrots, roughly chopped

2 celery stalks, roughly chopped

1 garlic bulb, skin on, split in half

100 g (3½ oz) tomato paste (concentrated purée)

1 bottle of red wine

2 bay leaves

2 rosemary sprigs

2 thyme sprigs

1 tablespoon black peppercorns

1 tablespoon juniper berries

Preheat the oven to 200°C (400°F).

Place the bones in a large roasting tin and into the oven. Roast the bones until they are golden brown, rotating them to colour evenly. This should take anywhere between 30 minutes to 1 hour.

Place the bones in a stockpot and set aside.

Add all the vegetables and the garlic to the roasting tin. Return to the oven and roast for another 20–30 minutes, until the vegetables have taken on some colour.

Remove from the oven and fold the tomato paste through, then roast for a further 15 minutes.

Remove the roasting tin from the oven again and deglaze with the red wine. Next, add the mixture to the bones. Pour in enough cold water to reach the top of the bones. Add the remaining ingredients and bring to the boil, constantly skimming the stock as it comes to the boil.

Once boiling, turn the heat down to a rolling simmer and cook for at least 4 hours. The lower and slower you can get the stock to simmer, the more flavoursome it will be.

Strain the stock, then let it cool down before storing it in the fridge, where it will last a maximum of 2 weeks.

It's a good idea to portion it down and freeze it, so you have access to good stock when you need it. It will last 6–12 months in the freezer.

JERKY

I like to do my jerky in my offset smoker, but you can also use your oven. If you are not using a smoker, many recipes will ask you to use 'liquid' smoke. I don't like liquid smoke for many reasons, so I recommend that if you are not using a smoker, don't worry about using liquid smoke, because the jerky will still taste great. The only tips I have for jerky are to use the leanest cut of meat – game topside works great – and to have the meat semi-frozen, which makes it easier to cut thinly, and when it fully defrosts, the moisture from the meat helps with the marinade.

You can also make jerky in designated ovens and dehydrators; I have never used these, so just follow the manufacturer's directions.

MAKES ABOUT 1 KG (2 LB 3 OZ)

1.5 kg (3 lb 5 oz) game topside, semi-frozen (remove your meat from the freezer 4 hours before working with it)

50 g (1¾ oz) Dry rub (page 209)

30 ml (1 fl oz) soy sauce

30 ml (1 fl oz) honey

a pinch of Cure salt #1 (see page 165)

Slice the topside as thinly as you can across the grain, then place in a bowl. Add the other ingredients and mix well. Marinade in the fridge for 12 hours.

When you're ready to cook, preheat the oven or your smoker to 80°C (175°F).

Remove the meat mixture from the fridge and place on a clean cloth to take up the excess marinade.

If you are using an oven, take the meat off the cloth and arrange the meat on a drying rack on top of a flat baking tray. If using a smoker, arrange the meat on the smoking trays. Make sure the meat is in a single layer, with no overlapping bits.

Place in your oven or smoker and cook for 40 minutes. Remove and leave to cool on racks, to ensure you get air underneath.

I find a clamp-down ring-sealed jar is best to keep the jerky in. It should keep for a few months; you will notice if it becomes too dry to eat.

A GUIDE TO FIELD DRESSING

A comment by my late godfather, Lyall Crockford, has always stuck in my mind: 'Once an animal is down, it grows twice in size and weight.' The hunting of game is a minor part, compared to field dressing and packing out an animal – with preparation being the key to success. The rewards are great, yielding fresh free-range organic protein.

FIELD DRESSING EQUIPMENT

Having a complete set-up when you harvest an animal is a must. There is nothing worse than having an animal down and not having the right tools for the job.

When I'm out in the field, I have a set-up for the job at hand and a back-up on me, and then I have another in the car. Yes, it sounds like overkill, but I like to have sharp knives when I need them.

Your field kit may vary depending on where and what you are hunting, if you're in the backcountry, or if you can get a car to the animal.

Here is a list of the gear that I have on hand, some with me and some at home; I mix-and-match it for the area that I am hunting in.

1 **Disposable gloves**
An easy way to keep your hands much cleaner, especially when you're out in the field.

2 **Game bags**
Go for good-quality game bags that seal up, so if you hunt in summer you are not battling flies. I have five 'quarter' bags in my day pack, measuring 43 cm × 73 cm (17 in × 29 in); the ones I have are breathable, so the meat cools and sets properly.

3 **Knives**
I always have two boning knives, one gut/tripe knife and a skinning knife, and one interchangeable scalpel knife. I have held a knife in my hand for my job since the mid-1980s, so I use commercial butcher or meat worker knives. I find I can keep them sharp and they clean well. I also find the blades are designed to do the job. The boning knives are for the first cut and meat removal. The gut or tripe knife is very handy with its reverse blade, so you are not cutting fur into the animal – and you can use it on the stomach and won't puncture the gut. The skinning knife is curved, and made for the job of skinning. I'll also take a small steel in my backpack to hone the knives if needed, and I keep a water stone at camp or in my car to resharpen the knives if I have to.

4 **A hoist and gambrel**
I have a compact field hoist and small stainless steel gambrel that I can pack with me to take into the field, to hoist the animal off the ground, up the side of a tree. Getting a carcass off the ground to dress it makes the job so much easier and cleaner. If you have access around where you are hunting, it's also great to be able to set it up at camp and dress the animal there. The meat also sets well, and being hoisted off the ground, you won't have an issue of anything helping itself to a feed in the middle of the night. Get one that you can set up at home or take with you – or a length of good rope, to help secure a large animal during dressing.

5 **Meat saw**
Use this for extracting the ribs, or jointing. I have a small one for my day pack, and a large one for home or camp.

Dry pluck

1. Hold the bird by the feet, and start to pull the feathers out against the grain. Do this with some pressure, but not excessive pressure, or you will rip the skin. Continue until done.

2. You can finish off all the little feathers with a kitchen blowtorch, then follow steps 4–6 in the wet pluck section.

‡ **NOTE**
Birds are better left all intact for a few days, and dressed after 5 days minimum. I store them in a fridge in a cardboard box.

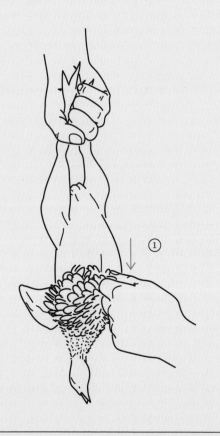

Wet pluck

1. Place a pot of water, big enough to submerge the bird, on a high heat, and bring the water to 70°C (160°F). (If you don't have a cooking thermometer handy, boil up some water, then add 2 parts boiling water to 1 part cold water in a separate pot, and that should be around the right temperature.)

2. Take the bird by the back legs and push it in and out of the water 25 times. This will make sure the water gets up under the wings.

3. Place the bird on a bench and start to pull the feathers out. If they are not coming out easily, give the bird another 10 plunges.

4. Once the bird is plucked, take a sharp knife and cut from the anus up to the back of the breast. Slide your hand into the cavity, up to the neck of the bird, and then grip and remove the innards.

5. Place the innards on your workbench and trim out the liver, heart and gizzard. (The gizzard is the muscle that grinds the grains and seeds that the bird eats, so it can digest the feed. The gizzard boils up a treat once you have split and cleaned it; then you can pickle it to keep it longer.)

6. If you can, hang your bird out until it is touch dry; on a nice winter's day, this should only take a few hours. If that is not possible, place it in the fridge with no covering, so it dries out.

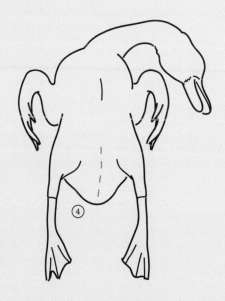

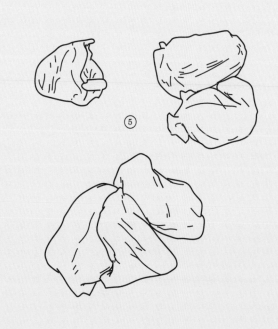

Small game animal field dressing

1. Hold the head up, with the bottom towards the ground, and place light pressure on the abdomen with your thumb. Stroke downwards and drain the animal of urine.

‡ **NOTE**
Sometimes it is better to leave the pelt on for transport in pieces, so the meat doesn't get dirt on it.

If you are not tanning the pelt

1. Take a sharp boning knife and remove the head, and front and back feet from the animal (see on right).

2. Pinch the fur in the middle of the back with your thumb and index finger, then make a cut through the fur.

3. Put your index and middle fingers into the hole, then pull in opposite directions to peel the fur back off the body. Once you reach the end of the carcass, place your hand in the middle of the body, then pull the fur over the end. Repeat on the opposite side.

4. Take your knife (making sure it's clean of fur) and make a shallow cut straight from the back end, down towards the rib cage.

5. Split the inside pelvis in between the back legs with your boning knife and remove the intestine and stomach (viscera) of the animal. It's okay to leave in the heart, liver and lungs until you do the rest of the cleaning at home.

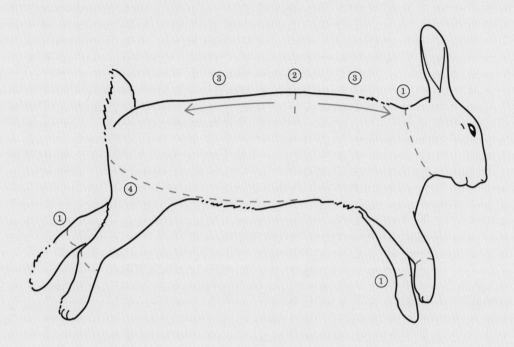

If you are tanning the pelt

1. After draining the animal of urine, make the slit from the back end straight to the rib cage as described in step 4 on the left page and eviscerate the animal. Hang the animal, or store it in a game bag until you get it home, to skin it for tanning (see tanning instructions on pages 112–3).

2. After skinning the animal, remove the heart, liver and lungs and inspect for any blemishes. Remove the gallbladder from the liver, and separate the heart, kidneys and liver.

3. Give the animal a rinse under cold water, pat dry and store appropriately. If you can hang the carcass free from touching anything, that would be best. The organs are best kept in a sealed container in the fridge.

‡ NOTE

Possum fur will slip or fall out while it's warm. In some countries, the animals are plucked for their fur, which is done while they are still warm. The fur is simply plucked out in clumps, to be used in yarn production, or mixed with merino wool and turned into warm, soft socks, beanies and jumpers. If you want to keep the skin intact to tan the possum hide, be very careful when handling the carcass, as the fur will come out if you pull at the animal. If you want to tan the hide, it's best to hang the animal whole overnight to let the fur set before handling.

1. Take a sharp knife –
   preferably a double-sided pig
   sticker (see note). Insert the
   knife from the Adam's apple,
   back towards the shoulders,
   and bring the knife back
   towards you, running it along
   the neck. (If you cut from ear
   to ear, blood will bleed back
   into the shoulders and ruin
   the meat.)

2. With a boning knife, make an
   incision around the anus. Pull
   it away from the sides, then
   tie a knot around the back
   passage/sphincter with twine
   or string. This will stop any
   faeces falling out when you
   are removing the intestinal
   tract from the pelvis.

3. Take the back trotter and cut
   lengthways up on the inside of
   the trotter, then cut on the
   other side, lifting the tendon
   up from the middle of the back
   of the trotter. Repeat on the
   other side. (This lets you
   hang it from your gambrel and
   still have room at the top of
   the leg.) Place your gambrel
   through the back legs and
   lift with your hoist to your
   desired height.

4. Make a small cut with your
   boning knife in between
   the legs, going through the
   belly into the stomach. Once
   through, place two fingers
   into the stomach and spread
   your fingers apart, while
   lifting them up. Reverse
   your knife with the blade up
   towards you (or use a gut/
   tripe knife) and cut down
   towards the sternum.

5. Once at the base of the
   sternum, cut the sternum
   toward the head; some people
   find this easier to do using a
   bone saw.

6. Place your hand up into the
   leg cavity and start to pull
   down on the anus, bringing the
   intestinal tract down. Then
   a couple of small cuts should
   bring all the internals out.

7. Place the internals on the
   ground and inspect for signs
   of disease, such as a blue
   tinge from 1080 poison (see
   page 62–3).

8. To skin the pig, make a small
   cut with the boning knife
   around the back trotter, then
   cut in towards the pelvis with
   your gut/tripe knife. Repeat
   the same step on the front
   trotters, cutting in towards
   the ribs.

9. With your skinning knife,
   start to cut the skin away
   from the carcass, starting
   at the top and peeling back,
   so you are not getting dirt
   onto the meat. Let gravity be
   your friend when taking the
   skin off.

10. Once skinned, wash the inside
    of the carcass if needed.
    Place in a cool room, or bag it,
    and let it set overnight.

‡ **NOTES**

A double-sided pig sticker is a
specialist knife that is long and
double-sided. The act of bleeding
a pig is called 'sticking', and the
technique is very different to
normal bleeding.

You can make prosciutto with
the hair still on the back leg.

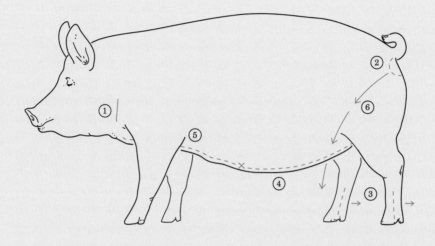

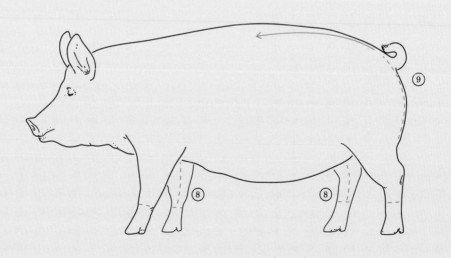

1. Take a boning knife and remove the head. For deer, if you want to cape the head, follow the instructions on page 142–3.

2. With your boning knife, make an incision around the anus. Using twine or string, tie a knot around the back passage/sphincter, to stop any faeces falling out when you pull the intestines out of the animal.

3. Using the same knife, make a cut down the inside of the back legs, towards the pelvis.

4. Open the skin of the legs, cut the join at the hock, and snap and pull down to expose the hocks. Cut in between the back tendon and leg. Place your gambrel through the tendon hole in the back legs and lift with your hoist to your desired height.

5. Using a skinning knife, cut the skin away from the pelvis and get it to the stage that it is down from the back legs. Using a gut/tripe/reversed knife, split the hide from the pelvis to the neck, making sure you don't puncture the stomach.

6. With your hand, start to punch the skin off the hide, through the middle and the back of the animal. Take a boning knife and cut the front hock back towards the rib cage, and clean the skin of the side of the hocks. Punch the skin off around the shoulders.

7. Take the skin at the top of the back legs, pull down with force, and it should rip down off the carcass; it might need you to cut a little as you do this. Rip the pelt from the carcass.

8. Start to make a small cut with a boning knife in between the legs, going through the belly into the stomach. Once through, place two fingers into the stomach and spread your fingers apart, while lifting them up. Reverse your knife with the blade up towards you (or use a gut/tripe knife), and cut down towards the brisket.

9. Once at the brisket, cut through to the throat, using your boning knife if it is sharp enough; some people find using a bone saw is easier.

10. Place your hand up into the leg cavity and start to pull down on the anus, bringing the intestinal tract down. A couple of small cuts should then bring all the internals out.

11. Place the innards on the ground and inspect for signs of disease (see pages 62–3).

12. Wash the inside of the carcass if needed. Place in a cool room, or bag it, and let it set overnight.

‡ **NOTE**

If you have access to a cool room where you hang the animal whole for ageing, you can gut the animal before you transport it, then do the skinning later.

Some of the larger deer varieties you will need to field dress on the ground (see pages 230–1), as they can be too big to lift. Take your time and transport the meat with the skin on to keep it cleaner until you are somewhere you can break it down.

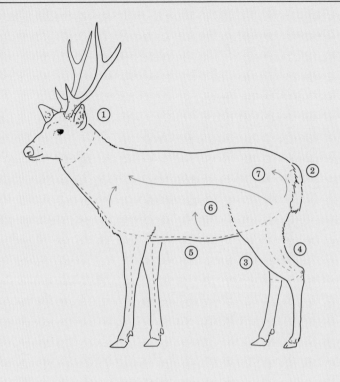

1. Take a boning knife and remove the head. (Unless you are caping the head, in which case follow the instructions on page 142–3.)

2. Then split the skin or pelt from the back of the neck, down to the pelvis.

3. Start to cut back the skin down towards the belly, removing the skin from the meat.

4. Using your boning knife, remove the backstraps, followed by the shoulder, leg, brisket and neck (refer to page 118 for the position of these cuts).

5. If you want to get the hanger, skirt and trim for sausages (for cut positions, see page 118), then it's best to gut the animal (follow the instructions for gutting deer on page 224, steps 2 and 8–11). Do this before removing these cuts.

6. Place the innards on the ground and inspect for signs of disease.

7. You can easily remove the beef tenderloin once the animal is gutted. Cut up on the inside of the backbone towards the pelvis and pull the tenderloin/eye fillet off the spine. Then cut it away off the bottom side of the loin.

8. Turn the animal over and repeat on the other side.

9. Once skinned, wash the cuts of meat if needed. Place in a cool room, or bag it, and let it set overnight.

‡ **NOTE**
This is an animal that you will most likely be field dressing on the ground, unless you have access to a tractor for hoisting. If you are lucky enough to have a tractor, skin the carcass as you would a wild pig (see page 222–3).

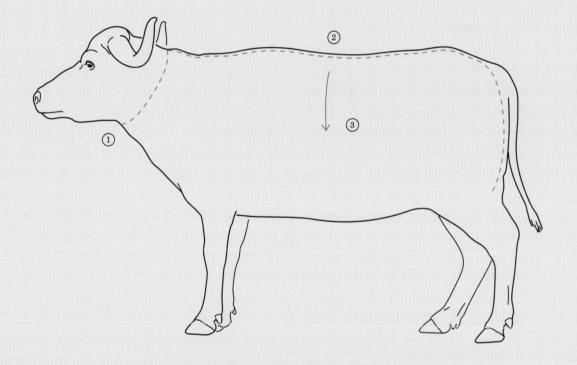

1. If possible, invert the animal on a shooting rack or hoist (or get your mate to hold the back legs). Take a sharp knife and stick it into the chest about 2.5 cm (1 in) under the front paws, about 5 cm (2 in) deep, then cut back towards the head, about 7.5–10 cm (3–4 in) long. This will 'heart stick' the animal and bleed it out properly, removing the blood pockets in the chest cavity.

2. After it has bled out, remove the head.

3. Take a sharp boning knife and cut around the anus. Then invert the blade (or use a tripe/brisket knife) and cut from the pelvis towards the rib cage.

4. Get your hands inside the cavity and pull out the innards. Inspect the offal for disease (see pages 62–3).

5. Make three cuts: one around the front paws, one around the back legs, and then cut from the tip of the tail, on the underneath side, up towards the pelvis.

6. Now cut from the front paws into the rib cage, and from the tip of the back legs towards the pelvis.

7. Start to cut the skin away from the tail. Once you have about 15 cm (6 in) of skin, pull the skin off the tail until it stops at the pelvis.

8. Start to cut the skin away from the back legs and the sides of the main cut, down from the pelvis. Pull the skin down the back, towards the front shoulders.

9. Skin the front shoulder, then punch the skin from the carcass.

10. Once skinned, wash if needed. Place into a cool room, or bag it, and let it set overnight.

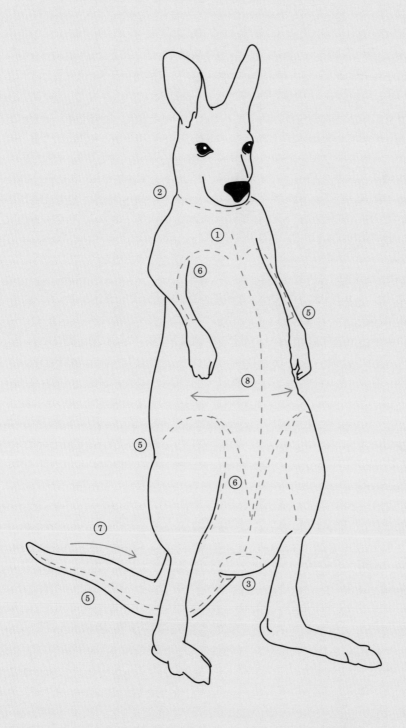

These instructions are for the larger species that you can't get out of the field whole, and you have to break them down and backpack them out. The gutless method can also make things a lot easier when you get the game home. I find the carcasses I leave in the field are cleaned up very quickly by birds and other animals, so are returned to the cycle of the bush. This relates to a lot of field hunting in remote areas, where you have to deal with the animal where it falls. Leaving the pelt on the outside of the meat of the legs and shoulders will help keep the meat clean during transport. It will also act as a barrier when you hang the legs to let them set and age and will prevent excess shrinkage and drying out.

1. Make sure the animal is well bled. Try to get the animal laying as evenly as possible on one side.

2. Cut the pelt from the back of the neck down the middle of the spine all the way to the pelvis area. This will help to start cooling the meat.

3. Cut a ring around the ankle of both the back and front leg.

4. If you are keeping the cape, cut down the middle of the animal so it splits the hide into 2 halves and then proceed to peel back the hide and cut towards the front ankles and 'sock the front legs', not splitting the hide.

5. On the back legs, cut from the spine down the outside of the leg towards the ankle and then proceed to cut back the hide from the flesh in all directions (this can also be done on the front if you are not taking a shoulder mount).

6. Once the hide is away, you can cut the shoulder off, then the leg, followed by the backstraps and neck. While doing this, place the meat into your game bag straight away so it doesn't get dirty. To remove the eye fillets, cut in at the saddle and follow it up the bottom side of the spine and then remove the eye fillet.

7. Once one side is done, flip the animal and repeat on the other side.

8. If you want offal and ribs, this is also a very easy way to collect it as it makes access easier.

INDEX

ACKNOWLEDGEMENTS

This book's draft was written just as COVID locked down the world, so this project has taken much longer than anticipated to finish. Many people have been a part of the long process, and a lot has changed over the years it took to get the book done.

Without Jane Willson, this book wouldn't exist. It was her commitment after our first meeting – three years before the book was commissioned – to get the project off the ground that gave it a chance. To the team at Hardie Grant, driven by Anna Collett: editing by Katri Hilden, design by Murray Batten, illustrations by Arthur Mount, and the recipe crew with styling by Lee Blaylock and kitchen work from Riki Niwa Whatuira (aka Sticky) – thanks so much for all the time you have put in. A massive shout out to the talented Adam Gibson for making this book come to life with his camera. You are a legend.

To the people in the Australian firearm industry: Josh Raymond at Raytrade, Sarah Price at Ridgeline, Johannes Hannes at Swarovski and The Rossi family and Elise Petterson from Beretta Australia. Thanks for all the advice and equipment that made this easier.

Thanks also to the Kirley family at Mansfield Hunting and Fishing.

A special acknowledgement to my godfather Lyle Crockford. We never did get to hunt together, but you sparked this passion in me all those years ago. And finally, to my beloved Emma, and my kids Felix, Finegan and Molly. For your constant support and freedom to hunt, cook and live this life with you all.

ABOUT THE AUTHOR

Ross O'Meara has been a chef for thirty-three years, and has lived in the US, UK, France, Asia and all over Australia. After several years pig farming on Tasmania's Bruny Island, he relocated to Mansfield, in north-east Victoria, with his wife and three children, to have access to hunting all year round. He is sought out by chefs and hunters across the country as a leading source of local knowledge in the field of game meat harvesting.

Ross is also known as one of three hosts of the long-running SBS television series *Gourmet Farmer*, with Matthew Evans and Nick Haddow. Ross appeared on several series, as well as being co-author of two cookbooks with Evans and Haddow: *The Gourmet Farmer Deli Book* and *The Gourmet Farmer Goes Fishing*.

Published in 2022 by Hardie Grant Books,
an imprint of Hardie Grant Publishing

Hardie Grant Books (Melbourne)
Wurundjeri Country
Building 1, 658 Church Street
Richmond, Victoria 3121

Hardie Grant Books (London)
5th & 6th Floors
52–54 Southwark Street
London SE1 1UN

hardiegrantbooks.com

Hardie Grant acknowledges the Traditional Owners of the country on which
we work, the Wurundjeri people of the Kulin nation and the Gadigal people
of the Eora nation, and recognises their continuing connection to the land,
waters and culture. We pay our respects to their Elders past and present.

 A catalogue record for this
book is available from the
National Library of Australia

Wild Meat
ISBN 9781 74379 640 5

10 9 8 7 6 5 4 3 2 1

Project Editor: Anna Collett
Editor: Katri Hilden
Design Manager: Kristin Thomas
Designer: Murray Batten
Photographer: Adam Gibson
Illustrator: Arthur Mount
Stylist: Lee Blaylock
Production Manager: Todd Rechner

Colour reproduction by Splitting Image Colour Studio
Printed in China by Leo Paper Products LTD.

 The paper this book is printed on is from FSC®-certified
forests and other sources. FSC® promotes environmentally
responsible, socially beneficial and economically viable
management of the world's forests.

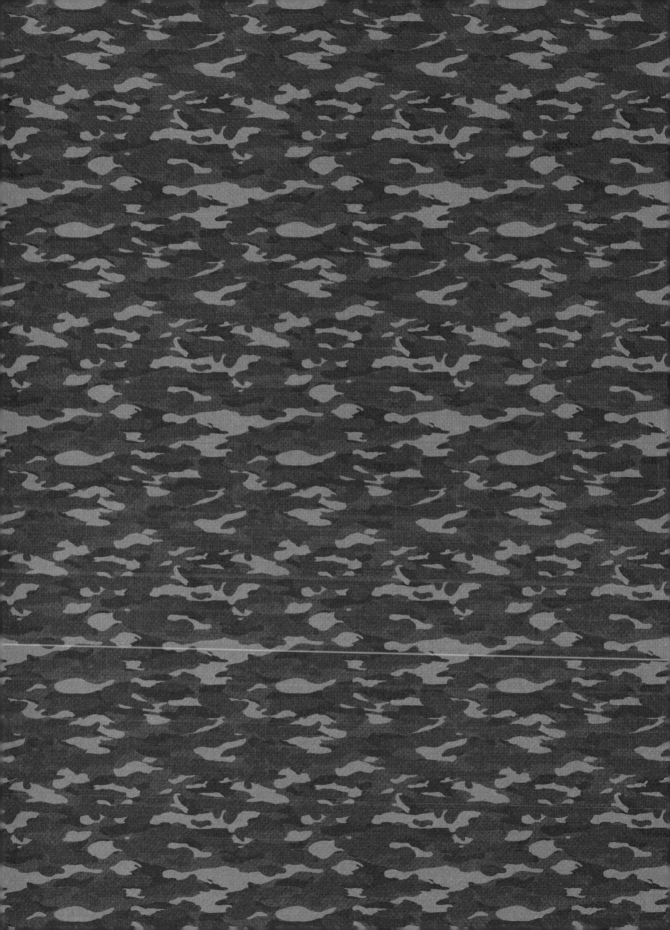